The Standard Model for Business

Know business better.
Do better business.

Edward Rowe

Rethink

First published in Great Britain in 2026
by Rethink Press (www.rethinkpress.com)

For Kristina, William, Maria, Olivia. There is no truer or greater purpose than to be the best man, husband and father for our family.

I hope William, Maria and Olivia read this book, giving them the best advantage in their future careers.

Contents

Foreword

Modern organisations are exceptionally complex systems. As they scale, leaders often find that intuition, functional excellence, or even deep industry expertise is no longer enough to understand why performance sustainably improves in some areas while it breaks down in others. What is usually missing is not effort or intelligence, but a coherent way of seeing the whole.

The Standard Model for Business addresses this problem directly.

Rather than focusing on leadership styles, motivational theories, or isolated best practices, this book offers a structured model for how companies are built, operated, governed, and assured as they grow. It provides a clear map of the core business functions, how they interact, and how their importance shifts across different stages of business maturity. In doing so, it helps explain many of the challenges that leaders face as companies evolve.

What I particularly value about this framework is its practicality. It does not assume perfect conditions, unlimited resources, or textbook businesses. Instead, it reflects the realities of modern enterprises: competing priorities, imperfect information, regulatory pressure, and the constant trade-offs between speed, control, and resilience. Readers will recognise the situations described because they live them every day.

This book is especially useful for professionals who want to move beyond their functional silo and develop a broader enterprise-level perspective. Wherever you work, understanding how the full system fits together is increasingly essential. Leaders who can see these interdependencies clearly are better equipped to make decisions that scale, rather than solve one problem while creating another.

What *The Standard Model for Business* provides is not advice, but orientation: a way to understand where an organisation is, how it is structured, and what tensions are likely to emerge next. It offers a shared language and a structured way of thinking about how businesses really work. For anyone serious about building, leading, or governing effective businesses, that perspective is indispensable.

Tim Breen, Chief Executive Officer, GlobalFoundries

Introduction

Business can feel chaotic, especially from the inside. In any company, large or small, every team speaks a slightly different language. Finance talks in margins and variances. Marketing speaks in funnels and conversion. Operations discusses throughput and downtime. Human Resources (HR) tell of engagement and capability. For Technology it is systems, data and integration.

Early in my career at Grant Thornton, back in 2004, I remember sitting in meetings and quietly writing down acronyms so I could look them up later. Everyone else seemed to know what was happening. I was determined to catch up, to understand how businesses really worked, not just in theory but in practice.

Over the next few years, I worked at KPMG before moving into industry, where I built and led the internal audit function for a distribution group operating across Western Europe. In 2010, I relocated to Abu Dhabi, joining one of the world's most sophisticated sovereign wealth platforms. Over the next fifteen years, I delivered assurance and risk oversight across portfolios that included aerospace, advanced manufacturing, renewables, technology, oil and gas, mining, financial services, healthcare and global investment vehicles. I am currently responsible for building the internal audit and risk management functions for a sovereign private equity firm with over $400 billion in assets under management.

Throughout my career I realised something fundamental: **There is no universal map of business.** There are excellent frameworks for strategy, for marketing, for operations, for finance and for leadership, but they sit in isolation. They explain slices of the business world, not the whole.

Executives learn through experience and trial and error. Entrepreneurs burn cash trying to scale because they're thinking about products when they should be thinking about partnerships, or they're thinking about marketing when they should be thinking about cash flow.

The business world has grown in complexity, but our frameworks have not grown with it. This book will change that.

Why I wrote this book

I wrote this book to offer clarity to anyone who has ever tried to understand how business really works.

Throughout my career, whether building internal audit and risk functions, advising audit committees or working alongside investment teams managing billions, I found myself returning to the same question: Why is the business world so difficult to understand from the outside yet so structured once you see how the pieces fit together?

The more I learned, the more I realised something important. Business is not chaos; it only feels that way when you cannot see how it all fits together.

I began to sketch a framework for my own use. Not a textbook, not a theory but a map. Over time, that sketch evolved into a simple, universal structure: five stages, twenty functions and a clear path for how businesses progress.

The more I used it, the more powerful it became. It helped me advise boards, coach teams and guide leaders through complexity. It gave me clarity in moments when everything around me felt uncertain.

I wrote this book to give you the same clarity and to provide a model you can use throughout your career, no matter your role, ambition or industry. I wanted to create the book I wish I'd had when I was starting out: practical, structured and written in plain language. *The Standard Model for Business* grew from years of experience, reflection and real-world lessons. Now it is yours to use, adapt and build upon.

How to use this book

I could not say everything I wanted to without turning this into a heavy textbook. That was never the goal. This book is meant to be practical, readable and immediately useful, not a doorstop that gathers dust.

I have focused on what matters most: the essential principles, structures, behaviours and practices that allow a business to operate at each stage of its life cycle.

For readers who want to explore deeper, every chapter includes a QR code linking to additional resources, templates and extended explanations. These free online materials expand each function without overwhelming the book. Think of this book as the map and the QR codes as optional field manuals.

Is this book for you?

I wrote this book for you, the **ambitious professional** who wants to understand business at a deeper, wider, more strategic level. You may be:

- **A manager or specialist** preparing to step into leadership and needing the breadth to think like an executive
- **An entrepreneur** building something exciting but overwhelmed by what to focus on next

Whatever path brought you here, you share one thing: ambition. You want to understand business well enough to navigate it with confidence, to contribute meaningfully and to build a successful career or company.

This book exists to give you the clarity that most people never have.

Business feels complex and it is. Truly. Every company is a collection of moving parts: ideas, systems, people, money, processes, risks and decisions all interacting at once. Without a clear framework, it feels messy and overwhelming.

Most business books focus on one topic (leadership, strategy, sales, culture or finance), which is useful but incomplete. It's like understanding one wing of a plane in detail and hoping the rest will make sense later.

There is no common model that explains business end-to-end, from the moment an idea sparks in someone's mind to the moment a company becomes a global, well-governed institution.

Until now.

A universal framework for business

The Standard Model for Business offers a clear, structured and universal framework that applies to companies of every size, sector and geography. It breaks down the business world into five developmental stages and twenty essential functions, all in plain, practical language.

This model gives you:

- **A map** of how companies actually work
- **A lens** to understand where your business is today
- **A guide** for how to move your business from one stage to the next
- **A vocabulary** to communicate confidently across departments
- **A foundation** to become a stronger leader or build a better business

The core aim of this book is to help you become a strong generalist.

A truth often missed is: **The best chief executive officers (CEOs) are rarely the deepest experts in any one function.** They are the best generalists; broad thinkers who can connect the dots, ask the right questions and understand how all functions interact.

This book is your introduction to that way of thinking.

The company life cycle

The chapters follow the life cycle of a company:

- **Chapter 1** introduces The Standard Model for Business, the five stages and twenty functions.
- **Chapters 2–6** explore each stage in depth: Start, Stabilise, Grow, Govern and Assure.
- **Chapter 7** explains how companies raise, manage and structure their financing as they move through each stage.
- **The Conclusion** brings everything together, showing how the entire model forms a coherent system for building, scaling and sustaining a business.

My goal is simple. I want to give you the clarity I wish I'd had early on in my own career and a way to see business as an integrated whole rather than a confusing maze.

If you understand this model, you will understand business far more quickly than most people ever do. You will see connections and patterns that others miss. You will speak the language of leaders. Most importantly, you will know how to build, grow and run a business with confidence.

Welcome to *The Standard Model for Business*. Let's begin.

CHAPTER ONE

The Standard Model

CHAPTER ONE

The Standard Model

I have always been a student of science. I loved the subject at school and ended up studying chemistry at University College London. At the start of my first year, I clearly recall attending a small group discussion with around four or five students and a professor in Philosophy of Science. During my degree I attended hundreds of lectures at university, but this single one stands out in my memory, twenty-five years later:

'You must understand that all science can only be explained in simple, human-made models of reality,' the professor said to me and the small group of students. 'Everything you have learned up to now is technically false, and everything you will learn in this degree is not reality.'

My jaw dropped as my paradigm was shattered in my mind. I asked tentatively, 'Can you explain?'

'Sure. In chemistry we think of solid, spherical atoms and molecules bumping into each other. In biology we think of complex molecules such as DNA dancing with other molecules in the miracle of life. In physics we think of protons, neutrons and electrons as solid, particle-like entities. Reality, however, is very different. You will learn quantum mechanics and discover that particles are not solid; they are wave functions that are probability densities. Even then, these models are approximations.'

Most of that went over my head, but I trusted him.

He continued. 'I'm sure you are all familiar with the periodic table in chemistry from high school.' I nodded approvingly, that *was* something I was familiar with. 'There is also something called The Standard Model of physics. The periodic table summarises all known elements in an easy-to-understand and reference framework. The Standard Model of physics summarises all known particles in the universe. These human-made constructs and models allow us to (more easily) understand and teach reality. The models allow the maths to work; actual reality would break our brains. The universe is a majestic sight, but at the smallest scales it is a mind-bending mix of incomprehension – too fast, too noisy, too unreal for us to fully comprehend.'

That day planted a seed: even the most complex systems can be simplified into useful models. When we had this discussion in 2001, the Higgs particle was not yet discovered, but it was added to The Standard Model of physics in 2012. The Standard Model of physics is incomplete and an approximation, but it is the best fit to describe the universe as we know it today, a simplification of reality that can be updated and changed as new evidence comes to light. Years later, I realised the same principle could be applied to business. As with The Standard Model for Business, I welcome review and challenge, and I can update the model as our understanding of business improves. One key area will be artificial intelligence (AI) and its impact on business. Today, AI is quickly becoming an integral part of business, and in the near to medium future it has the potential to completely upend business models and how businesses are structured. At that point, The Standard Model for Business will, of course, be updated.

Fast forward twenty-five years to the present day, I draw many parallels between these scientific models and business. Companies and the business they conduct are highly complex entities, operating in a complex world. Finding a way to simplify this so that they are easily understood became a personal mission. CEOs and business leaders do this intuitively, balancing complexity, making trade-offs and seeing the bigger picture. That is why I created The Standard Model for Business; a way to make sense of the complexity and the sheer scale of modern business. Like The Standard Model of physics, it may not capture every nuance of reality but it gives us a framework to work with, to cut through the noise and to act with confidence as we navigate our business journeys.

Just as my professor once revealed a model that changed the way I saw the universe, I'd like to reveal one that will change the way you see business. In this chapter, you'll learn about the components of The Standard Model for Business and how you can use it to know business better and do better business.

Why The Standard Model for Business?

This book is for the ambitious professional who doesn't want to wait ten years to 'figure out' how business really works. *The Standard Model for Business* is your shortcut.

- **For professionals.** It helps you rise beyond your silo, think like a CEO and accelerate your career.
- **For entrepreneurs.** It shows you the functions you'll need to scale.

Most people, including myself, stumble through by trial and error, learning painfully slowly. This book cuts through the noise by breaking down business into a structured framework that is simple to grasp and powerful to apply.

Don't just take my word for it. Jeff Immelt, former CEO of GE, is attributed with saying, 'The most valuable business skill is to be able to connect the dots between seemingly unrelated ideas.'[1] Lou Gerstner, former CEO of IBM reiterates this: 'You can't deliver value unless you connect the dots across the entire company.'[2] That's what this book is about – helping you build the breadth and perspective to connect the dots across functions, industries and people. If you don't know the dots, it's hard to connect them. You need to have knowledge across all areas, as management thinker Peter Drucker emphasises: 'The manager of the future will have to be a very knowledgeable generalist, with a grasp of the essentials across many areas.'[3]

If you still need convincing that generalists succeed, let's look at the data:

- **Broad skills outweigh specialisms.** *Range* by David Epstein[4] argues that people who develop broadly – exploring multiple skills, domains and experiences – ultimately outperform specialists in solving complex, unpredictable problems.
- **Most CEOs have experience in multiple different roles.** The average CEO held nine roles across seven companies before reaching the top, usually spanning multiple functions. *DDI Global Leadership Forecast 2018*[5] surveyed 25,000 leaders in 2,500 organisations across 54 countries and identified cross-functional general management

as the most common stepping stone to becoming CEO.

- **Business leaders and entrepreneurs are overwhelmingly generalists.** A 2018 *Harvard Business Review* analysis of 17,000 CEOs worldwide[6] found that over 90% had broad general management backgrounds rather than narrow functional expertise. Edward Lazear's 'Jack-of-all-trades' theory[7] used US labour market data to show that individuals with diverse work experience are significantly more likely to become entrepreneurs. Stuetzer, Obschonka and Schmitt-Rodermund[8] replicated this in German data, confirming that entrepreneurs are disproportionately generalists.

- **Generalists have a problem-solving edge.** In 2015, Melero and Palomeras[9] analysed tens of thousands of inventors in the electronics industry. They found that generalists contributed disproportionately more to teams facing novel, uncertain problems, helping overcome coordination challenges by drawing from broad knowledge bases.

- **Generalists improve business outcomes.** The *O.C. Tanner Global Culture Report 2023*,[10] a survey of 36,000 workers in twenty countries, showed that when generalists were empowered to use their breadth, companies saw +114% higher likelihood of revenue growth and were twenty-six times more likely to report a thriving culture.

Introducing the model

The Standard Model for Business is designed to be a universal framework that explains how companies are put together, providing the ambitious professional with a structured way of understanding all the moving parts of a business. Similar to a conductor and their orchestra, with each corporate function being a different instrument with its own characteristics, tone and rhythm, the model shows how harmony is achieved when every function works together.

Without this coordination, the result is noise and confusion, which I experienced when I started my career. Just like the best CEOs and business leaders, The Standard Model for Business is industry agnostic; you can apply this across all industries as it is designed to be a general framework for business generalists. Throughout my career I have seen the same principles being applied across all industries, without exception.

Becoming a generalist is hard to achieve. You need to understand at least 80% of the detail within all functions in a business to be a good generalist, one that can hold their own with functional specialists. Our education systems and training programmes tend to push people to specialise. This is great at the start of your career or when building a business, as focus is needed. However, as the overwhelming statistics suggest, having a general grounding in business is beneficial for business leaders and becoming a great CEO. Being a specialist in one or two functions is not good enough.

The model focuses on the technical understanding of business and companies; this is not a framework for soft skills and leadership. There are many books and frameworks on these topics out there for you already, created by extremely experienced and skilled leaders. The Standard Model for Business ensures a general, rounded knowledge of all areas of a business, allowing you to understand holistically the inner workings of a company, regardless of its size or positioning.

You may be thinking, 'Why do I need this? Can I just "wing it"?' To an extent you could, and I have seen many people try to do this, but it is never a successful strategy in the long term. You will be caught out by the many specialists and smart people that you come across, and any gaps in knowledge will become painfully apparent. The right path is harder but backed by knowledge and understanding.

The Standard Model for Business is organised in two levels:

1. **Stages.** There are five stages of The Standard Model for Business, taking you on a journey through the life cycle of all companies, from a start-up to a large, listed (on a stock exchange) company. The five stages are: Start, Stabilise, Grow, Govern and Assure. I'll provide an overview of each stage in the next section.

2. **Functions.** As part of the model, each stage has three, four or five functions within it. There are twenty functions in The Standard Model for Business, and these functions are represented by the coloured boxes in the diagram. Each box is colour-coded to represent the stage to which it belongs, allowing for easy navigation.

While no two companies are identical, The Standard Model for Business can be applied across industries, sectors and geographies. This book will cover the five stages and provide an overview of the twenty functions. I condense over twenty years of corporate experience into an easy-to-digest, simple model, which serves as a development tool, helping ambitious professionals to think as strong generalists, to think like a CEO. By understanding business holistically, you can avoid siloed thinking and instead make better, more informed decisions throughout your career.

Ultimately, The Standard Model for Business is not theory for theory's sake. The model is a practical playbook, a way to diagnose weaknesses, guide strategy, design training and benchmark best practices. Just as the periodic table organises chemistry and The Standard Model of physics organises the universe, The Standard Model for Business seeks to organise the complexity of modern enterprise into a clear, structured and usable form.

The five stages

Let me take you on a tour of the model. Each of the five stages represents a phase in the life of a company. Each stage is supported by a set of functions, and they create a full map of modern business:

1. **Start.** Turning an idea into reality. Creating a product or service, finding customers and proving you have something worth buying. Fast decisions, blurred roles, limited resources. The challenge: finding a product–market fit.

2. **Stabilise.** Bringing order to chaos. Building systems and functions – finance, HR, information technology (IT), legal, comms – that create the foundation for sustainable growth.

3. **Grow.** Scaling up. Expanding products, services and markets with ambition and discipline. Research & development (R&D), partnerships, logistics; functions that create momentum and reach.

4. **Govern.** Protecting performance. Procurement; administration; quality, health, safety and environment (QHSE); and corporate governance ensure efficiency, discipline and accountability as the stakes rise.

5. **Assure.** Securing trust. Risk; ethics & compliance; environment, social, governance (ESG); and internal audit provide confidence to stakeholders that the company is not only effective but responsible.

How to read the model

The Standard Model for Business should be read from top left to bottom right:

1
Start
The core

The top left is **Start**. This is the core of every business, revenue generation. **Stabilise** is wrapped around the core of the business to stabilise the core.

2
Stabilise
Protect the core

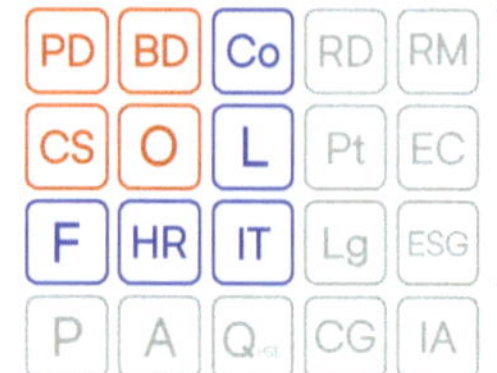

Surround the core business with stabilising functions

3
Grow
Expand the core

Expand the core business and stabilising functions with grow functions

Grow is across the core and stabilising functions, to grow the entire business.

4
Govern
Sustain the core

Sustain the core business, govern the stabilise and grow functions with governing functions

5
Assure
Sustain the business

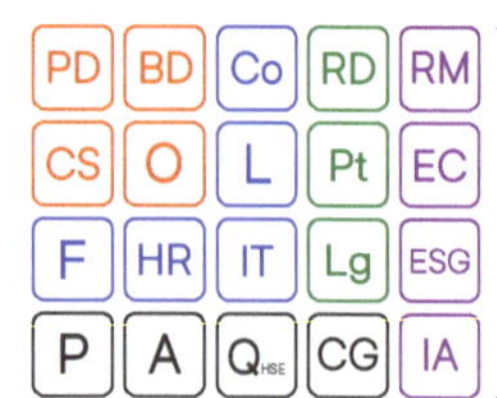

Provide Assurance to stakeholders across all business functions

Govern is across stages **Start**, **Stabilise** and **Grow**, to ensure the entire business is managed effectively. **Assure** is across all business functions, ensuring the business is sustainable in the long-term.

QUESTIONS FOR YOU

1. How do you currently see business? As a collection of separate functions or as one interconnected system?
2. How does The Standard Model for Business compare to your company's structure? Do you recognise the five stages?
3. Where do you place yourself today? Are you a specialist in one area or do you already have some generalist breadth? How do you think that has shaped your career so far?
4. Have you ever felt siloed or limited by your perspective? What opportunities might be revealed if you could connect more dots across functions?
5. Think back to your own education and early career. Were you encouraged to specialise or to broaden your understanding? What impact has that had on your journey? If you had a model that simplified business into a clear framework, how might that change your confidence, decision-making and ability to lead?
6. Imagine you are a CEO today. Would you feel prepared to discuss and make decisions across finance, HR, procurement, risk and strategy, or would there be gaps in your knowledge that you would worry about?

Take some time to reflect on what you have learned so far.

Summary

This chapter began with a lesson from science: that all our understanding of the world is built on models; human constructs that simplify complexity into something we can all work with. Just as the periodic table organises chemistry and The Standard Model of physics organises the building blocks of the universe, so too can business be simplified into a structured model. The Standard Model for Business introduces a practical framework to help you cut through the noise and make sense of the complexity of modern companies.

I propose that while the most successful business leaders and CEOs are natural generalists, balancing complexity and joining the dots, most of us need a structured way to learn and build this skill. The system tends to push us into narrow specialisms, which are useful early on but can be limiting in the long term. The data presented shows that generalists, not specialists, are more likely to occupy the most senior positions in business and more likely to succeed as CEOs, entrepreneurs and problem solvers. By developing a broader knowledge base across business functions, the ambitious professional can accelerate their career, build credibility and trust, and avoid pitfalls such as siloed thinking.

The Standard Model for Business provides this breadth in an accessible way. The model is organised into five stages – Start, Stabilise, Grow, Govern and Assure – and together they reflect the life cycle of a company. Ambitious readers can learn and use this model to begin to think more like CEOs, not only understanding their own area of expertise but also seeing how the wider company fits together.

The Standard Model for Business is both a time saver that accelerates your understanding of how companies operate and a compass that guides you through the complexity of how companies evolve over time. This is a practical book, designed to give you clarity, confidence and a generalist's edge in a specialist-driven world.

In the chapters ahead, we will step through each stage in detail. Naturally, we begin where every company begins: Start.

CHAPTER TWO
Start

CHAPTER TWO

Start

'You need a PhD to understand this stuff,' the finance manager said, implying I was out of my depth. 'This is the world's most complicated production process, with around 800 steps. The key is lithography. Each machine costs about $80 million. Do you know what a lithography machine is?'

'Yes,' I said. 'It projects light through a patterned mask onto a photosensitive chemical layer, shrinking the pattern to nanometre scales and etching transistor structures into the wafer.'

The manager stayed silent. I continued: 'At 12 nanometres and below you need extreme ultraviolet light. You generate this by hitting droplets of molten tin with high-energy lasers to create a plasma that emits short-wavelength UV light. Lithography is the bottleneck in the process, the rate-limiting step that drives yield and cost.'

The finance manager leaned back, reassessing. 'Yes. That's right.'

We shook on a deal. I would support their business planning and in return I could shadow engineers and tour the fabrication plant. What followed was the most impressive demonstration of business I have ever seen.

The product development department was my first stop. Whiteboards overflowed with the latest from

R&D: sketches, schematics and rough product ideas. The team debated the next product. Only a handful of ideas moved forward, shaped by solid engineering. Innovation here wasn't free rein creativity, it was structured and disciplined.

Next, I met the design team. Their screens showed microchip layouts resembling futuristic city maps. Every transistor placement had consequences; power consumption, heating, feasibility to produce, speed and performance. What struck me was the sheer scale of the engineers' designs. Computer-aided design squeezed billions of transistors onto a chip the size of a postage stamp.

The product managers worked with a wall covered with Post-It notes: faster speeds, lower power, industry certifications. They needed to decide which demands could be delivered. They co-designed products with larger customers, sharing early prototypes and shaping specifications together.

I realised that business development wasn't only about selling what the fabrication plant already made; it was about listening, predicting and aligning future technology with the market needs.

In the customer service department, managers discussed a product issue. When microchips rolled off the line, they weren't perfect. Some were defective, the yield was lower than usual. Field engineers were sent to customers, working with them until the problem was fixed. I realised customer service was as critical as the silicon itself.

The fabrication plant itself was inspiring. I put on cleanroom gear and stepped into a cathedral of technology of pristine air, humming automation and robots shuttling semiconductor wafers through the 800-step manufacturing process. We reached the lithographer, which was the size of a bus, performing just one task. It was automated choreography at scale.

The lesson was clear. Beneath the technology, automation and complexity, the fundamentals of the business were all there. The industry might have been semiconductors, but the lessons were universal, matching the four functions of the Start stage:

1. **Product development** is creativity within constraints.
2. **Business development** means aligning ideas with real market demand.
3. **Customer service** builds loyalty by ensuring customers succeed.
4. **Operations** turn vision into reality, at scale.

That is what the Start stage – the first stage in the model – is all about. Start is core to business; it turns an idea into reality. Let's go into each function in depth.

Product development

Without a product or service, a business is not a business. Every company must solve a problem. The challenge is to create something others will pay for.

Product development is comprised of four units: **ideation**, **design & engineering**, **product management** and **product launch**. Let's look at each in turn.

Ideation

Ideation is the creative, structured process of coming up with ideas to address a problem, testing those ideas and developing a product or service, ready to go to market.

Most ideas will fail along the way and the best ones evolve from the carnage of failure. The healthiest approach is to let the best idea win. An inclusive culture is crucial; even the least-experienced member of the team can contribute.

An effective creative process incorporates divergent and convergent thinking. Divergent thinking is opening up the realm of possibility, brainstorming and exploring the art of the possible, and pushing the boundaries of what is commonly accepted. Convergent thinking narrows down this wide range of ideas into feasible options. Successful businesses balance both types of thinking.

Common tools in ideation include:

- **Customer feedback.** Speaking directly to customers to understand their needs and problems.
- **Brainstorm workshops.** Defining problems, generating ideas and using divergent thinking.
- **Market research.** Reviewing trends, competitors and technological shifts.
- **AI.** Large language models (LLMs) are increasingly being used to generate ideas.
- **Idea development.** Convergent thinking focuses on the most promising ideas. A feasibility lens is held up against each idea.

A key outcome of ideation is a pipeline of potential concepts. Only a few ideas will move forward to design & engineering.

Design & engineering

The challenge becomes turning an idea into something real and ready for the market.

The design process ensures that the idea is captured on paper; that the product is usable, ergonomical, appealing and aligned with expectations. The engineering process ensures that the product (or service) can actually be built, scaled and delivered reliably.

For physical products, this involves materials, prototypes, technical design and manufacturing. For services, it includes process mapping, service blueprints, creation of digital assets and the use of technology. For software, it is coding, system architecture and system design.

A common pitfall here is 'over-engineering'. It is not necessary to have the perfect product before going to market.

Best practice encourages rapid prototyping and iteration. A minimum viable product (MVP) is built quickly and cheaply and tested with customers, feedback is gathered and the product improved. The lean-startup methodology developed by Eric Ries popularised this principle: 'Build, measure, learn.'[11] Iteration is the key: fail fast, learn, improve.

Elon Musk's SpaceX[12] culture perfectly demonstrates this, where rockets are pushed to their limits and fail but the company collects a huge amount of data to learn from, and overall progress from failure to success is faster than their competitors.

Strong design and engineering balances quality and cost. With limited resources, companies need to prioritise. Do they:

- Use premium materials?
- Use cheaper alternatives that make early production feasible?
- Design a beautiful product?
- Make design compromises to mass produce at scale?

These choices are strategic decisions that underpin the success of the product or service.

Product management

Product management ensures the product or service is produced in the right way, for the right customer needs and evolves over time as needs change. It defines the vision for the product, creates a product development roadmap, sets priorities and aligns cross-functional teams around delivery.

An effective product management discipline includes:

- **Product vision and strategy.** How does this product fit into the company's vision, mission and strategy? Does it fit the current product portfolio or is it a new innovation that could cannibalise the current business but lead to long-term value?
- **Product development roadmap.** Sequencing features, updates, releases and versions. A planned product development roadmap allows the company to realistically deploy new products to market, based on the resources available.
- **Managing trade-offs.** Balancing customer needs, engineering capacity and commercial realities. The company must make a profit from the product or service being developed.
- **Feedback loop.** Listening to customers, sales teams and customer support. Analysing the feedback and feeding it into product development on a continuous basis.
- **Product performance.** Revenue generation, adoption rates, customer satisfaction, customer churn. Analysing data enables smarter product decisions and quick pivoting if the product or service is not working as intended.

Without effective product management, a lack of coordination can lead to chaos. Product management is continuous. Products and services have a life cycle of introduction, growth, maturity and eventually decline. Managing when to invest, when to improve and when to retire is key to long-term profitability.

Product launch

This is the moment when the initial idea meets the market as a product or service. Remember, an MVP is sufficient to begin with, so long as it meets the regulations of your industry. This allows the company to go to market quickly, get customer feedback and pivot accordingly. It is this lean and agile approach to product development that provides a competitive advantage.

A successful product launch involves:

- **Positioning and messaging.** Clearly articulating what the product is, who it is for and why it matters. The company's marketing function is needed here. (We will talk about marketing in the next section of this chapter.)
- **Go-to-market planning.** Creating a single plan to align sales, marketing, distribution and product support to launch effectively.

- **Pricing.** Deciding how to capture value from the product or service, whether through premium positioning, penetration pricing, freemium tiers or subscription models. This choice sets expectations for customers and signals the company's market intent.
- **Channel readiness.** Preparing how the product reaches customers (including training distributors), ensuring retailers understand the value proposition or setting up a website.
- **Customer onboarding.** Making the experience simple, smooth and engaging for customers. This reduces friction, builds confidence and trust in the product and lays the foundation for long-term loyalty.

A poor product launch can doom even the best products. History is filled with excellent products that failed due to weak marketing or timing.[13] With the right launch, even modest products succeed, creating excitement, scarcity and momentum in the market.

Post-launch feedback from customers is critical. Early users reveal issues, highlight missing features and suggest improvements. Companies that treat launch as the start of an ongoing dialogue, rather than the finish line, are those that sustain success.[14]

Business development

Business development is the art of coordinating sales, marketing and branding; the engine that drives your business forward. It tells a compelling story about your business that converts interest into loyal customers. Strategy is at the core; a clear vision effectively executed is critical to success.

Business development has four units: **sales, marketing, brand & positioning** and **vision, mission & strategy**.

Sales

Sales is the process of converting interest into paying customers. It is building relationships, telling stories, persuading customers and closing deals. Sales converts interest into revenue and is critical to the success of a business.

An effective sales process is built on four principles:

1. **Listening before speaking.** Understanding the customer's pain points before pitching a solution. This can only be done by listening first. A potential customer may not be best serviced by your product, and that is OK. Telling them so builds trust in you and your brand.

2. **Communicating value.** Explaining what the product is and how it solves the customer's problem. Storytelling is important here. Simon Sinek's *Start with Why*[15] articulates this point wonderfully. *Why* builds an emotional connection with the customer, rather than just providing specifications of the product.

3. **Trust-building.** Credibility, reliability and follow-through matter more than flashy persuasion. It is not just a transaction, it is building a strong relationship between you and the customer.

4. **Persistence and resilience.** Rejection is common in sales, but consistency leads to breakthroughs. It is a numbers game: the more people in your sales funnel, the more you will convert into paying customers. Particularly when starting out, small companies need to go through hundreds of 'noes' to get a single 'yes'.

Regardless of which channel the company uses, sales is about building strong relationships with people.

Customers buy from brands and people they trust and believe in.

Marketing

Marketing is the process that generates initial interest in your product or service. Sales is one-to-one, while marketing is one-to-many. Marketing amplifies awareness, generates leads and sets the stage for sales. It is how you broadcast your story to the world in a way that resonates with your chosen audience.

Good marketing starts with clarity: *Who is the target customer and what matters to them?* Understanding this enables precise articulation of your offer, why it matters and how it is different from alternatives. The clearer and more compelling the message, the more likely it is to cut through the noise.

Marketing broadly consists of two areas:

1. **Inbound marketing.** Creating value so that customers come to you. This includes building excellent products and the brand and reputation that follows, content, blogs, videos and social media. This creates authority and trust.
2. **Outbound marketing.** Actively reaching out to prospects through advertising, events, cold outreach or partnerships. This is faster than inbound marketing but requires precision

(ie targeting the right potential customers) to avoid wasted cost and effort.

The key objective for marketing is to create a flow of interest; potential customers that the sales team can engage with and convert. An effective marketing function reduces the cost of acquiring a customer (or customer acquisition cost), reducing the barriers to sales conversion and increasing the lifetime value of a customer and profitability.

Brand & positioning

Brand is one of the most important but underrated aspects of business. Brand is not just a logo, a colour palette or a tagline; it is the perception of your company in the minds of your customers. Positioning is how you shape those perceptions: the space you occupy in the market relative to competitors. Together, brand and positioning define who you are, what your values are and why customers should choose you.

A brand must be intentionally built. This involves:

- **Clarity of promise.** What does your company consistently deliver?
- **Consistency of experience.** Every interaction with customers, whether it be your website, packaging or customer service, can reinforce or damage your brand.

- **Differentiation.** How do you stand out from your competitors? On price, quality, design, innovation or values?
- **Emotional connection.** Customers don't just buy products, they buy meaning. How does being aligned to your brand feel for the customer?

Positioning requires strategic choices. Are you the premium option or the affordable alternative? Are you serving a niche or aiming for the mass market? These choices influence everything, from pricing to marketing tone to sales channels.

A strong brand and clear positioning create trust. New customers will take a risk on your company if they perceive professionalism, reliability and alignment with their values. Weak branding creates confusion and hesitation and therefore undermines sales.

Vision, mission & strategy

A core element of business development is the mandate and direction of the company: the vision, mission & strategy:

- **Vision** describes the desired future state of a company. This is typically 10+ years in the future, difficult to achieve and designed to inspire.
  A strong vision inspires employees, attracts like-minded customers and entices investors.

- **Mission** defines why the company exists – its purpose. It should detail what the company is doing every day to fulfil its vision.
- **Strategy** is a defined plan for how the company will fulfil the mission and vision, detailing action plans that the company can execute.

Without a vision or mission, there is a lack of cohesion and nothing to aim for. Companies are rudderless. With all three elements in place, business development becomes not just about selling a product but about building a company that customers, employees and partners want to join and support.

Customer service

Acquiring customers is just the start; retention builds a sustainable business. Outstanding customer service converts one-time buyers into long-term, repeat and loyal customers. It builds reputation and brand, strengthens customer relationships, rectifies complaints and rewards customer loyalty. Companies that master customer service build robust communities that cannot be easily replaced or broken by competitors. Customer service can be broken into four key areas: **customer service centre, complaint resolution, customer relationship management** and **retention & loyalty**.

Customer service centre

The customer service centre is the first port of call for your customers. It is the 'first impression' customers have of your company. In the past, customer service was a dedicated call centre. Today, it may also include email, live chat, AI chatbots, social media or a website.

A well-designed customer service centre provides a seamless way for customers to get information. During every interaction, a customer forms an impression of your company. Helpful, prompt and empathetic customer service builds trust. Slow, confusing or indifferent service erodes it.

Customer service centre good practices include:

- **Multi-channel access.** Communication preferences can vary from customer to customer. Different channels include online, telephone, mobile, live chats and social media. Be as accommodating as possible.

- **Information management.** Clear and easy-to-reach documentation reduces customer frustration and improves consistency.
- **Training.** Customer service staff should be highly skilled and trained communicators with a detailed understanding of all products and services.
- **Metrics.** Use of key performance indicators (KPIs) to track response times, resolution rates and customer satisfaction. KPIs help monitor performance of the customer service centre.
- **Automation with a human touch.** Over-automation of customer service can be frustrating for customers. Automation ensures efficiency and effectiveness, but a human in the loop is needed to build and maintain the relationship with the customer.

Outstanding customer service is a differentiating factor for companies. We can all think of a company that provides great customer service; their reputation is highly regarded with strong customer loyalty.

Complaint resolution

Complaints are inevitable. What matters is how your company handles them. Complaint resolution is about demonstrating accountability, care and empathy while also fixing the problem.

A poor experience will drive customers away. A positive experience strengthens customer relationships. Customers will tell others of their experience, whether good or bad. They will judge your company on the quality of its response and how it makes them feel during the complaint process.

Effective complaint resolution involves the following four steps:

1. **Active listening.** Customers want to feel heard before they want solutions. The customer service team should demonstrate that they have heard the customer.
2. **Acknowledgement.** Your company should lead and acknowledge responsibility for the problem, even if the issue is complex. The company must avoid deflecting or blaming others.
3. **Swift resolution.** Time matters, and delays compound customer frustration.
4. **Follow-up.** The customer service team should check-in with the customer after resolution to confirm satisfaction.

Effective complaint resolution is powerful. Referred to as the 'service recovery paradox',[16] customers who experience a problem that is quickly resolved can become more loyal than those who never had an issue.

Good processes, the ability to escalate quickly, empowered employees and a human touch are critical for complaint resolution. If every decision requires an approval by a manager, resolution will be slow. Empowering customer service employees to make reasonable decisions builds confidence and trust on both sides.

Customer relationship management

Customer relationship management (CRM) goes beyond an individual customer interaction. It is a systematic approach to understanding, tracking and nurturing the relationship with each customer.

CRM often refers to an IT system that helps manage customer information, eg purchase history, preferences, log of interactions and feedback. Effective CRM puts the customer at the forefront of the business.

Strong CRM enables the following:

- **Personalisation.** Tailoring offers, communications and services to individual needs. This makes the customer feel special and listened to.
- **Proactivity.** Anticipating customer needs before they arise. This is made easier via data analytics. Data-driven decision-making helps you to manage customers more effectively.
- **Cross-selling and up-selling.** Identifying opportunities that genuinely add value to

customers but also add value to the company's bottom line.

- **Effective targeting.** Segmenting your customer base allows you to distinguish between high-value customers, occasional buyers and at-risk accounts. Tailoring your approach to these groups allows you to maximise the opportunity, by generating more revenue from your best customers, and by converting *on the way-out* customers to brand ambassadors for your company.

CRM requires significant alignment throughout the business to be effective. Technology is useless if staff do not record interactions or act on insights. A commercial approach and customer-centricity must be embedded throughout the business, including culture, processes, incentives and decision-making.

Retention & loyalty

Retention & loyalty programmes ensure that customers stay, return and deepen their relationship with your business. Repeat customers increase the lifetime value of a customer, providing more revenue for the same cost to acquire that customer, driving efficiency and profitability.

Customer retention starts with consistent delivery, which builds trust over time, creating loyalty and building an emotional connection.

Below are some customer retention & loyalty approaches:

- **Loyalty programmes.** Discounts, points (such as airline points) or rewards for repeat purchases.
- **Exclusive experiences.** Early access, VIP events or insider content.
- **Community building.** Creating spaces (online or offline) where customers connect with each other and the company.
- **Recognition.** Acknowledging high-value and long-term customers with personalised messages or offers.

Discounts and special offers may be appreciated by the customer, but true loyalty arises from shared values, trust and identity. Successful brands cultivate communities of customers who identify with the brand's ethos as much as the products and services on offer.

Operations

Operations turn promises into reality. It is the behind-the-scenes world of production, projects, supply chains and support services. Failure to deliver what was promised can lead to reputation damage, reduced sales, increased complaints and even bankruptcy. Strong operations build reputation and trust that keeps customers coming back.

Operations can be divided into four essential areas: **production**, **support services**, **project management**, and **supply chain management**.

Production

Production is the process of creating the product or service, turning raw materials into finished products, where code is developed, tested and deployed or content is created.

The main objectives of production are consistency, efficiency and quality at the right cost. Robust, often automated production processes ensure that high-quality products are made, current demand is met, and the process can be scaled as demand grows.

The key considerations for an effective production process are:

- **Capacity.** Balancing supply and demand. Too little capacity loses potential sales, with potential damage to reputation with stock-outs. Too much leads to idle capacity, excess capital expenditure and reduced prices. The best scenario is to produce *just less* than market demand.

- **Quality.** High-quality products build trust in your company. Quality control implements checks and standards to detect any defects during production. Automation helps here where consistency is needed.
- **Cost control.** If costs are out of control, a company loses money on each product or does not make enough revenue to cover the high-cost base. A cost-efficient production process is the foundation for a profitable business.
- **Flexibility.** The ability to adapt production to new models, features or customer requirements. In recent decades, mass customisation has developed as a means to satisfy the varying needs of the customer.

Production is about trust. Customers will return only if they believe the product will deliver every time.

Support services

Support services can be core or ancillary to a company's revenue generation. Ancillary services tend to support a product and can be significant, eg car finance, maintenance, insurance customisation, warranties and subscriptions.

Support services are delivered in real time, often directly to the customer. This makes consistency harder to manage, as every interaction heavily relies on people, relationships and context.

To deliver a high level of support service that is scalable, your company should focus on the following areas:

- **Standardisation.** Repeatable processes to ensure every customer receives a consistent experience. Standardisation helps to ensure employees execute a repeatable process every time.
- **Training.** Employees need to be equipped with both technical and interpersonal skills. Trust is built with credibility (knowledge) and clear communication.
- **Scalability.** Ensuring the service expands to meet demand without collapsing under strain. Automated services help scalability, as more users are added to an app or system.
- **Feedback.** It is essential to create a feedback loop where lessons are learned and fed into the service process to improve it. This culture requires constant discipline to review processes and continuously improve.

Support services succeed when they balance effectiveness with human relationships, delivering at scale while making each customer feel valued.

Project management

Every business must deliver projects, eg launching a new product, building a website, opening a store or implementing a new IT system. Projects are temporary – with defined beginnings and ends – and are critical to operations.

Project management ensures projects are delivered on time, on budget and at high quality. Project management brings structure to complexity, breaking work into tasks, sequencing them and effectively managing available resources.

Key elements of effective project management are:

- **The project management triangle.** This shows the tension between cost, time and scope. These three areas determine the quality of the project's deliverables. Since resources are limited, trade-offs are required. To maintain high quality, only one area can be compromised. With a limited budget, you can reduce the scope or increase the time the project takes. With limited time, spending more for the same scope will ensure you deliver on time.
- **Clear objectives.** Everyone must be aligned with what success looks like. This is essential for the project manager to effectively lead and deliver the project.

- **Planning.** Project planning includes defining project scope, setting key milestones and allocating resources. This allows the project manager to forecast if the project is feasible given time and resource constraints (refer to the project management triangle above).
- **Execution.** The project team needs to effectively communicate to coordinate tasks, manage dependencies and pivot when problems arise.
- **Monitoring and control.** The project manager should track progress, address project risks and resolve issues as they arise.
- **Closure.** Ensuring the project delivers its intended value, with lessons learned captured and actioned for future projects.

Project management approaches vary, from traditional 'waterfall' methods with sequential phases to 'agile' approaches with an iterative process.

Poor project management can waste time and money, and lead to the company missing its objectives. Effective project management demonstrates that the company is organised and can deliver.

Supply chain management

No business operates in isolation. Supply chain management coordinates materials, components, logistics and external partners to ensure consistent and reliable delivery.

As a business grows, it expands to global sourcing, multiple suppliers and logistics networks, ensuring you have enough stock to meet demand. (We will go into this in detail later in 'Logistics' in Chapter 4, and 'Procurement' covered in Chapter 5.)

The key objectives of supply chain management are:

- **Availability.** Ensuring the right materials, components or services are delivered when needed.
- **Cost optimisation.** Balancing quality with affordability.
- **Resilience.** Having other options if suppliers fail or disruptions occur.
- **Transparency.** Knowing where your supplies come from and how they are produced.

Today, supply chains are increasingly scrutinised for ethics and sustainability. Customers and regulators want assurance that products are made responsibly, without exploitation or harming the environment. Companies that ignore this risk damage to their reputation and loss of trust.

Technology provides real-time inventory tracking, predictive analytics and blockchain-based traceability. Essentially, supply chain management is about relationships: trust and collaboration with suppliers, partners and distributors.

QUESTIONS FOR YOU

1. If you stripped your business back to its first principles, how would you clearly and confidently describe the single problem you exist to solve? How does your product or service do this better than anyone else?
2. Are you building with inspiration or with discipline? What would change if you achieved the perfect balance between the two?

Take some time to reflect on what you have learned so far.

Key learnings

1. **Products and services**
   All businesses start with a problem to solve and a product or service to sell. Quality and fit with customer needs are the foundation on which everything else rests.
2. **Developing your business**
   Define a clear vision, mission and strategy that everyone can buy into and repeat.
3. **Looking after your customers**
   Customer care means building lasting relationships. Listening, personalising, resolving complaints quickly and rewarding loyalty turns first-time buyers into lifelong advocates.

4. **Running the show**
   Operations turn promises into reality through efficient, scalable systems that balance quality, cost and capacity. Effective operations manage risk, ensure ethical supply chains and drive continuous improvement.

Final thoughts

For more details and free content on the Start stage, please visit Standardmodelforbusiness.com or scan the QR code:

Before moving on, pause and consider. The clarity and inspiration you build in the Start stage will become the core of your business, profoundly defining everything that follows. Now comes the need for discipline, creating the systems, processes and consistency that allow your business to operate with seamless repetition and form the foundation to scale. We now turn to Chapter 3: Stabilise.

CHAPTER THREE

Stabilise

CHAPTER THREE

Stabilise

'Are we in control?' the CEO asked. The question came halfway through the executive meeting. Around the table, each department head looked to the next: finance, HR, IT, legal and communications. Each confident in their own area but uncertain of the whole.

The business was performing well. Revenues were strong, customers were happy and operations were expanding. Yet something wasn't right. Reports were inconsistent, staff turnover was rising, IT issues were mounting and contract renewals were being missed. Together, these issues pointed to a deeper problem.

I was brought in to lead an entity level controls audit; a review of how the business governs itself.

On the surface, everything looked fine – policies, systems, capable people – but beneath it each department worked in silos and made decisions without coordination. The company was busy but not in control.

Finance was diligent but reactive. Reports arrived late, reconciliations were rushed and forecasts were inaccurate. We introduced a financial close calendar, clear responsibilities and a single version of truth in the IT system. Soon, month-end became a predictable process. Forecasts improved. Finance stopped reacting and started planning.

HR policies existed but were poorly communicated. Hiring and onboarding was inconsistent and performance reviews were irregular. We created a policy register for the company's intranet. Job descriptions were refreshed and onboarding standardised. HR began quarterly engagement surveys with staff. Culture became consistent and people understood what was expected of them.

IT was functional but fragile, with shared passwords, infrequent backups and broad access rights. We implemented role-based access, tested backups and disaster recovery, and tracked issues through an IT helpdesk. Service levels were measured and a change-management process was implemented. Downtime fell and confidence grew.

Legal lacked control over contracts. They were scattered across folders, inboxes and shared drives, unsigned, outdated or missing. We set up a central contract repository, and standardised templates and renewal reminders. Procurement and legal developed approval thresholds.

Communications were fragmented. We introduced a communication ethos with weekly leadership updates, a monthly town hall meeting and a clear internal newsletter. Information became consistent, transparent and timely.

Six months later, the company was transformed. Month-end financials closed in half the time. Audit issues fell. Staff turnover declined. Contract disputes were reduced. People trusted information again. When the CEO asked again, 'Are we in control?' everyone was confident.

I learned that stability doesn't come from bureaucracy, it comes from consistency. It's about knowing who does what, when and why. That is what the Stabilise stage is all about.

The Stabilise stage establishes the structure and consistency for sustainable growth. Building systems, processes and disciplines brings order to the chaos. Finance, HR, IT, legal and communications become essential functions ensuring resilience, control and clarity so the business can move forward with confidence and survive.

The Stabilise stage has the following functions: **finance**, **HR**, **IT**, **legal** and **communications (comms)**.

Finance

Finance is the language of business, telling a story of where the business was, how it is and where it can go. From accurate records to planning cash flow and funding growth, finance brings structure and discipline, providing clarity and insights that leaders need to make informed decisions.

Finance combines four units: **accounting & tax, financial reporting, financial planning & analysis** and **treasury**. Together, these build the financial foundation that allows your company not just to survive but also to grow with confidence.

Accounting & tax

Accounting is the foundation of finance. It is the recording and presentation of every financial transaction: income, expenses, assets and liabilities. Reliable records are vital. Investors, auditors, regulators and managers rely on accurate accounting to understand what is going on in a business. Therefore, understanding financial statements is a significant advantage in the business world.[17]

In practice, accounting covers:

- **Bookkeeping.** Recording transactions consistently through a small online accounting system for startups, with a monthly fee, or enterprise-grade systems for large companies such as SAP or Oracle. This is called the 'general ledger'.

- **Accounts payable and receivable.** Businesses must bring in more cash than they spend to avoid too much debt and bankruptcy. Efficient cash management minimises time for customer receipts and maximises time for supplier payments, while optimising good relationships with both.
- **Payroll.** Ensures employees are paid correctly and on time.
- **Tax compliance.** Calculating and filing taxes accurately, on time and in line with jurisdictional requirements.

New companies sometimes fail to set aside sufficient funds for sales tax, value added tax (VAT), corporation tax or payroll taxes. Mature finance functions anticipate taxes as part of cash planning, not as an afterthought.

Accounting is sometimes dismissed as backward-looking and only relevant to accountants; however, without solid accounting and tax, every forecast and decision is built on a fragile foundation.

Financial reporting

Financial reporting translates the raw data of transactions (general ledger) into structured, standardised statements that explain financial performance and position. Having the ability to read financial statements is a great advantage as they show how well your business has performed.[18]

The three core financial statements are:

1. **Income statement or profit & loss (P&L).** This shows revenues, costs and profit or loss for the previous year or a specific period such as a quarter.
2. **Balance sheet.** This shows the financial position – assets, liabilities and equity of a company – on the day at the end of its financial year. It balances assets versus liabilities and equity:

   Assets = liabilities + equity

   An asset is something the company owns. A liability is something the company owes. Equity is the money put in by shareholders; another form of liability that the company owes to the shareholders.
3. **Cash flow statement.** This tracks the movement of cash in and out of the business over the previous year or period, such as a quarter. This is the most important of the three main financial statements, as a business lives or dies by the amount of cash it has left over. There are three main types of cash flow: operating, investing and financing. Free cash flow (FCF) is an important metric as it measures cash available for debt repayment, dividends or reinvestment:

   FCF = operating cash flow – capital expenditure

Good reporting is timely, accurate and in line with financial statement regulations. The best finance functions repeatedly ensure reports are produced quickly, checked thoroughly and communicated clearly.

Many stakeholders (investors, lenders, analysts, management, regulators, suppliers, customers) depend on accurate financial reporting. Poor reporting erodes confidence; clear, reliable reporting builds trust and opens the door to capital and opportunities.

Financial planning & analysis

Financial planning & analysis (FP&A) is the discipline of budgeting, forecasting and scenario analysis. FP&A asks:

- What do we expect to happen in the next quarter, year or five years?
- What resources will we need to achieve our objectives?
- What risks could prevent this, and how do we prepare?

A budget sets targets. Forecasts predict the near future to aid strategic decision-making. Scenario planning explores 'what ifs'. For example, what if sales fall by 20%? What if raw material prices double? What if we expand into a new market? Forecasting forces leaders to think through assumptions, priorities and trade-offs.

Modern data analytics and AI-driven models enhance FP&A. The fundamentals, however, are constant: clarity, discipline and foresight.

Companies that neglect FP&A risk overtrading; growing sales faster than working capital, leading to a cash crunch. Others expand into new markets without assessing the true costs, experiencing heavy losses. Effective FP&A reduces these risks and enables bold but calculated growth.

Treasury

The focus of treasury is to manage the company's cash, funding and financial risk. It is often overlooked in smaller businesses but becomes critical as a company grows.

Treasury covers:

- **Cash management.** Ensuring sufficient liquidity to pay bills and invest in opportunities. Importantly, large cash deployments typically require treasury approval, adding an additional layer of security for big investments.
- **Banking relationships.** Negotiating credit lines, loans and services. Strong relationships

with banks improve access to capital, reduce borrowing costs and provide vital support during economic downturns. (For more detail, see Financing in Chapter 7.)

- **Funding strategy.** Deciding whether to use equity or debt, in which proportion, aligned to the strategy of your company. An optimal funding mix balances growth potential with financial stability.
- **Financial risk management.** Hedging against currency or interest rate exposures. Proactive management of financial risks protects profitability and ensures that market volatility does not disrupt long-term strategic objectives.

For growing companies, effective cash management is critical. Treasury guides financial choices. Should you raise venture capital, take on bank debt or bootstrap growth? Each has implications for control, cost and risk. Strong treasury management weighs up these options with a clear understanding of trade-offs.

Treasury also guards against complacency and builds resilience against credit crunches or currency swings.

Human resources

Companies are only as strong as their people. HR unlocks talent, shapes culture and ensures people are trained and motivated to perform. Great HR attracts, retains and inspires top talent to build a better future.

When starting up, HR is often improvised. Founders hire friends, family or whoever is available, leading to undefined roles and responsibilities, informal employment contracts and culture develops by accident rather than by intention. This does not provide a stable platform for sustained growth.

The Stabilise stage professionalises HR by creating structures and processes that unlock talent, manage employee relationships fairly, reward contribution and ensure compliance with the law.

HR is composed of four units: **talent management**, **employee relations**, **compensation & benefits** and **policies & compliance**.

Talent management

Talent management is about finding, developing and retaining the people who will move the business forward. In small businesses, this responsibility likely falls to the founders. As companies grow, talent management becomes a dedicated discipline.

Key elements of talent management include:

- **Recruitment.** Hiring the right people requires clear roles, a structured interview and assessment process, and a strong cultural fit. A poor hire can be catastrophic, draining morale and resources.
- **Onboarding.** Proper onboarding ensures the employee knows what is expected of them, integrates them into the company's culture and ensures they are productive from day one.
- **Training and development.** Businesses that invest in learning modernise their workforces, build capability and signal commitment to employees' futures.
- **Performance management.** Formalising a performance culture across the company is important. This ensures accountability and

continuous improvement, fairness for all employees, that contribution is well rewarded, alignment of individual goals with organisational objectives, and fostering a sense of ownership and motivation throughout the workforce.

- **Succession planning.** Identifying and preparing future leaders ensures continuity and reduces disruption when key people leave.

In essence, talent management is about realising potential. Do we have the right people to achieve our strategy? If not, how do we develop or acquire them?

Employee relations

Employee relations builds and maintains the day-to-day relationship between the company and its employees. Successful employee relations help build a high-trust environment for employees, leading to better performance.

Employee relations covers:

- **Communication.** Employees want to understand decisions, strategy and their role within the company. Regular dialogue builds trust and alignment with the workforce. A lack of communication can lead to rumours and disengagement.

- **Employee engagement.** Beyond salary, people seek recognition, purpose, respect and belonging. Employee engagement includes surveys, focus groups and open forums to help leaders understand morale and act on feedback.
- **Culture development.** Culture is the sum of its behaviours. HR shapes and reinforces values, norms and standards that define 'how things are done here'. This includes recognising positive behaviours, ensuring leaders model company values and embedding cultural expectations into recruitment, onboarding and performance management. A strong culture fosters trust, accountability and shared identity.
- **Conflict resolution.** Disagreements are inevitable. How they are handled sets the tone for the company. Fair, transparent processes prevent disputes from festering.
- **Change management.** An important part of employee relations is managing change with the workforce, particularly changes that directly impact employees.

Businesses that neglect employee relations often suffer from low morale, high turnover and a poor reputation. Companies that invest in it create loyalty and discretionary effort. Employees go beyond what is required because they believe in the company, have a purpose and trust leadership.

Compensation & benefits

Compensation & benefits is how companies pay their employees. Remuneration must be correctly structured to attract and retain talent, align with performance and remain affordable and sustainable for the company.

Key considerations include:

- **Base pay.** Salaries should be fair, in line with employment law, competitive in the market for that skill set and consistent across similar roles. Pay inequity is not only illegal, it also quickly undermines trust between employees and employer.
- **Variable pay.** When designed correctly, bonuses and incentives should link rewards to performance – particularly long-term performance (multi-year) – helping to align employee effort with business results. Poorly designed variable pay schemes, however, can encourage the wrong behaviours, including excessive risk-taking and short-termism.
- **Benefits.** Health insurance, pensions, annual leave, flexible working and wellness programmes all contribute to how employees perceive the value of working for your company.
- **Recognition.** Non-financial rewards, such as awards, thank-you notes or career opportunities, reinforce a positive culture of celebrating success.

Compensation communicates what a business values. Generous parental leave signals commitment to families. Pay that is linked tightly to clearly measurable performance signals a meritocracy.

The challenge is balance. Paying too little risks losing talent. Paying too much will strain the company's finances. Strong HR functions use benchmarks (both in the market and internally) and performance metrics to strike the right balance.

Policies & compliance

Many people policies are driven by employment law. Multinational companies need to navigate multiple jurisdictions and employment laws. They may feel restrictive but they enable trust and protect the business from unnecessary risk.

Key areas include:

- **Employment law.** Contracts, working hours, leave entitlements and termination processes must meet jurisdictional requirements.
- **Health & safety.** Employers have a duty of care for their employees. Policies, training and monitoring protect employees and reduce liability.
- **Equality and diversity.** Anti-discrimination policies, inclusive hiring and fair treatment are

not only legal requirements in many jurisdictions but are also morally correct in today's world.

- **HR system.** Enterprise Resource Planning (ERP) systems integrate HR data such as payroll, time management, benefits and compliance reporting into a single system. A well-configured ERP system automates policy enforcement (such as leave entitlements and approvals), and reduces compliance risk through accurate, auditable records.
- **Documentation.** Employee handbooks, codes of conduct and disciplinary procedures provide clarity to all employees.

There is a trade-off between being small and nimble and large and stable. Large businesses are built for stability. Systems, policies, procedures and documentation all contribute to this stability.

Information technology

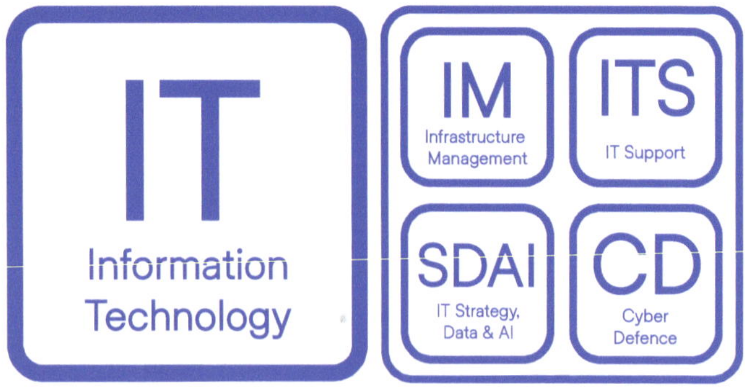

IT is the backbone of every business. Systems, big data and tight security enable a business to operate at scale. An effective technology strategy can turn efficiency into a competitive advantage. Whether it is deploying AI, automating tasks, protecting against cyber threats or using data to drive better decisions, IT creates momentum for the business. Without it, businesses fall behind in a digital-first world.

IT has four key units: **infrastructure management**, **IT support**, **IT strategy data & AI** and **cyber defence**.

Infrastructure management

Infrastructure is the foundation of IT. It includes the networks, servers, devices and cloud services that keep the business connected and operational. Ensuring capacity, stability and 'uptime' of the company's network are the key priorities.

Core responsibilities of infrastructure management include:

- **Hardware and devices.** Ensuring employees have reliable IT equipment to work productively.
- **Networks and connectivity.** Providing fast, secure and resilient internet and intranet connections.
- **Cloud services.** Managing platforms such as Amazon Web Services, Microsoft Azure or Google Cloud.

- **Business continuity.** Implementing data backups, disaster recovery and ensuring redundancy.

Weak infrastructure leads to downtime, frustration and lost productivity. Strong infrastructure ensures the business operates without interruption. As a company grows, investment in IT infrastructure is not optional, it is the foundation for everything else to scale effectively.

IT support

IT support is the face of the IT function. It is what employees turn to when something goes wrong. Access issues, software glitches, broken laptops; all issues are dealt with by the IT support team.

IT support is vital to employee productivity and morale. A single IT issue can paralyse someone's workday. Multiply that across your business, and poor support can cost a lot in lost time and productivity.

Key elements of effective IT support include:

- **Helpdesk systems.** Ticketing platforms to track and resolve IT issues efficiently.
- **Response time metrics.** Service-level agreements (SLAs) measure how quickly problems are acknowledged and solved by IT support.

- **Knowledge bases.** Self-service resources that reduce reliance on IT support staff. These are typically IT policies, procedures and FAQs, located on the company's intranet site.
- **Customer service mindset.** Treating employees as valued customers, which builds a strong reputation for the IT function and trust among employees.

When IT support works well, it becomes seamless and invisible. Problems are resolved quickly, employees trust the system and productivity is maintained at a high level. When it fails, frustration spreads and technology becomes a barrier instead of an enabler.

IT strategy, data & AI

Technology can be a strategic driver. Companies that treat IT only as maintenance miss opportunities to innovate. In the Stabilise stage, IT begins to influence the direction of the business through strategy, data and AI.

IT strategy aligns technology with business objectives. What systems do we need to support growth? How do we digitise processes? Where can automation save time and cost? Strategic IT investment can differentiate a company, creating new capabilities competitors cannot easily copy. IT strategy is about enabling the business to work smarter, faster and more competitively.

Data management turns information into an asset. Every company generates data, from sales and marketing to customer service and operations. Without the discipline and systems to collect, clean and analyse it, this data goes to waste. With good data, leaders can make smarter, faster decisions.

AI and automation are now within reach, even for smaller businesses. Chatbots streamline customer support. Machine learning models improve forecasting and predict demand. Generative AI helps with content creation and idea generation. AI will be transformational, but do not rely on it as a panacea to all problems.

Cyber defence

As businesses digitise, the risk of a bad actor gaining access grows. Strong cybersecurity is essential – one of the highest risks to a business in today's data-driven world. A single breach can expose sensitive data, damage customer trust, destroy your reputation in the market and lead to regulatory penalties.

Cyber defence covers:

- **Access control.** Ensuring only authorised users access systems.
- **Threat monitoring.** Detecting suspicious activity before it escalates.

- **Patch management.** Keeping software and systems updated to close vulnerabilities.
- **Incident response.** Having clear plans for when (not if) a cyber-attack occurs.
- **Training.** Equipping employees to recognise phishing, social engineering and other threats. Often the weakest point of entry to most companies are their employees. Clicking on the wrong link or a suspicious email attachment can lead to a hacker gaining access to your systems.

Stabilising IT means putting in place the controls, monitoring and culture to defend against these risks. Regulators are also tightening requirements. Data protection laws (such as the General Data Protection Regulation – GDPR in Europe) impose strict obligations on businesses to protect personal data. Non-compliance carries heavy fines.

Legal

A legal function protects the business from unnecessary risk. Contracts, compliance and regulations may feel like guardrails, but they are also enablers, creating the confidence to expand, partner and grow. A strong legal function prevents costly mistakes, safeguards reputation and ensures the company plays by the rules of its industry and jurisdictions. A well-protected business is a confident business.

Legal broadly covers four areas: **contract management, dispute resolution, intellectual property management** and **regulatory affairs**.

Contract management

Contracts are the backbone of business relationships. They define the rights and obligations of both parties, from suppliers and customers to employees and partners. Contracts ensure that both parties clearly understand their obligations and disputes are resolved quickly and amicably.

Effective contract management involves:

- **Drafting and negotiation.** Contracts must be clear, fair and aligned with business objectives. Negotiation skills are essential to balance risk and reward.
- **Standardisation.** Using contract templates for common agreements improves consistency and reduces risk of a contracting error.

- **Execution.** Ensuring contracts are properly signed and stored and are accessible. Lost paperwork or unsigned terms can invalidate agreements.
- **Monitoring.** Contracts should be actively monitored, not forgotten in a drawer. Are suppliers delivering on time? Are customers paying as agreed? Are contract renewal dates tracked?

Contract management systems automate tracking, deadlines and obligations.

Poor contract discipline leads to revenue leakage, supply chain breakdowns or exposure to liability. Strong contract management provides clarity and predictability in every business relationship.

Dispute resolution

Even with the best contracts, disputes can occur. Suppliers fail to deliver, customers default on payments, employees raise grievances or partners disagree. How your company handles disputes says a lot about its maturity and values.

Dispute resolution can take several forms, in order of time and cost:

- **Negotiation.** This is the fastest and cheapest method, where parties find a compromise directly, without using a mediator or the courts.

- **Mediation.** A neutral third party is appointed by both parties to help facilitate an agreement.
- **Arbitration.** Using lawyers as an arbitrator, this is a private, binding resolution outside the courts.
- **Litigation.** Court proceedings, often expensive and time-consuming, with the outcome legally binding.

The choice of method depends on the stakes, the jurisdiction and the relationship between the two parties. Disputes can drift into litigation if all other methods fail. Many contracts now include dispute resolution clauses that specify preferred methods, such as arbitration in a neutral country.

Key principles of effective dispute resolution include:

- **Communication.** Keep a line of communication open with the partner. Dispute resolution is a form of negotiation, and good communication is key to a successful outcome.
- **Preparation.** Thorough records are needed as high-quality documentation often determines outcomes.
- **Proportionality.** A company needs to weigh the cost of the dispute against the potential benefit. Not every battle is worth fighting.
- **Reputation.** Companies need to consider how aggressive legal action may impact brand perception or future relationships.

Companies with mature legal functions establish clear escalation processes for disputes, empowering managers to resolve smaller issues early while involving legal professionals for higher-risk disagreements. The goal is always to resolve fairly, efficiently and with minimal disruption to business.

Intellectual property management

Intellectual property (IP) is one of the most valuable assets a company owns. Logos, brand names, designs, inventions, code and proprietary processes all provide a competitive advantage; however, without protection, they are vulnerable to theft or being copied.

IP management covers:

- **Trademarks.** Protecting names, logos and brand identity.
- **Patents.** Securing exclusive rights to inventions and innovations. This encourages R&D and innovation, as patenting a new discovery allows the owner to economically benefit from the investment made.
- **Copyright.** Covering original works such as written materials, music or software, protecting it from being copied.
- **Trade secrets.** Protecting confidential processes, formulas or industry know-how.

A strong legal function ensures IP is identified early and is appropriately registered and defended, protecting and strengthening the company's reputation.

Companies must avoid infringing others' IP. Lawsuits for trademark or patent violations can damage a business. Due diligence is essential before launching products, brands or campaigns, to avoid infringing any existing IP.

Regulatory affairs

Every business operates within a framework of laws and regulations, which vary by industry, jurisdiction and size of company, but all carry obligations that must be met. Regulatory affairs navigates this complexity.

Key areas include:

- **Regulatory filings.** Filing annual returns, maintaining document registers and complying with company law.
- **Industry-specific regulations.** From financial services to healthcare, energy to telecoms, each sector has its own rules that must be complied with.
- **Data protection.** Regulations such as GDPR require strict controls over personal data.

- **Environmental standards.** Increasingly, companies must measure and report on sustainability metrics.

Effective regulatory affairs map out requirements, assign ownership to management, and implement strong monitoring systems. Compliance is embedded into processes. This reduces the risk of fines or reputational damage.

Regulatory expertise also enables growth. A company that understands compliance can confidently expand into new markets, attract investors and win contracts that require rigorous standards.

Communications

How a company communicates shapes how it is seen by customers, employees, investors and the wider world. Effective transparent comms builds trust, clarity and storytelling, thereby enhancing reputation. Internal comms gives employees a shared vision.

Communications covers four units: **external communications, internal communications, digital & social media** and **communication strategy & governance**.

External communications

External communications manages how a company interacts with the outside world through press releases, media relations, investor communications and brand storytelling. The goal is to shape perceptions, build credibility and protect the reputation of the business.

Core responsibilities include:

- **Media relations.** Building relationships with journalists and editors, providing accurate, relevant and timely information to the media.
- **Press releases.** Announcing news in a way that is professional, concise and aligned with brand messaging.
- **Investor communications.** Improving confidence among shareholders, analysts and lenders through clearly communicating updates and transparency.

- **Public affairs.** Engaging with regulators, government and community stakeholders to enhance the reputation of the company.

Poor external communications lead to confusion, mistrust or reputational damage. A single careless comment can undermine years of brand building. Strong external communications reinforce the company's market position and creates goodwill in times of crisis.

Internal communications

This is where a company's leadership must align all employees to ensure a happy and productive workforce. Employees need to understand the company's strategy, goals and values. Without clarity, even the best teams can become fragmented.

Internal communications covers:

- **Leadership messaging.** Ensuring business leaders communicate consistently and transparently about priorities, changes and results.
- **Channels and tools.** From emails, intranet, Teams and Slack to town halls and team meetings, all communication channels should be used for important announcements.

- **Employee engagement.** Communication is two-way. Employees should have forums to ask questions, raise concerns and share ideas. Senior management should listen to this feedback and act upon the best ideas.
- **Cultural reinforcement.** Stories, employee recognition and a shared culture helps to embed the company's values into the business.

The importance of internal communications is often underestimated. Many businesses assume employees 'just know' what is happening. Silence can lead to rumours, disengagement and mistrust. Well-designed internal communications ensure that employees feel informed, trusted, connected and valued.

Digital & social media

Today, a significant amount of communication is online. Social media platforms, websites, blogs and digital newsletters are often the first point of contact between a business and its stakeholders.

Responsibilities in this area include:

- **Content creation.** Developing posts, articles, videos and graphics that engage audiences.
- **Channel management.** Understanding which platforms matter for which audiences. LinkedIn for professional updates, Instagram for visual

branding, X (Twitter) for rapid commentary, Facebook for communities and TikTok for younger audiences.

- **Monitoring and engagement.** Tracking what is said about the company and responding appropriately. Effective social media is a conversation, not a one-way communicator.
- **Crisis response.** Digital platforms spread bad news quickly. A protocol for rapid, clear responses is essential.

Digital and social media give smaller businesses global reach at low cost, but they also carry risk to reputation. A poorly timed post or insensitive comment can escalate into a crisis. Digital channels should be treated as strategic assets, managed with care and professionalism.

Communications strategy & governance

A communications strategy ensures all communication from and within a company is clear, consistent and aligned to its values. Governance ensures that all communications, whether internal or external, are consistent, aligned and accountable.

Key elements include:

- **Core narrative.** An effective narrative can define the company's story – its vision, mission, values and positioning – ensuring it runs through every communication the company makes.

- **Tone of voice.** This is part of the company's brand. Tone of voice establishes guidelines for language, formality and style so that all communications 'sound' like the company and are aligned to its brand.
- **Approval processes.** Ensuring sensitive communications (eg financial results and crisis statements) are reviewed and approved at the right level, before communication goes out.
- **Policies and training.** Setting clear rules for employee communications, particularly on social media, and providing training to avoid any missteps.
- **Performance measurement.** Tracking communication effectiveness through surveys, engagement metrics and monitoring media.

Strong communications strategy & governance prevents mixed messages and protects reputation. It also ensures that when a crisis arises, for example a product recall, data breach or regulatory investigation, the company speaks with one clear, coordinated voice.

QUESTIONS FOR YOU

1. What systems, processes and disciplines does my company have that allows the business to run consistently?
2. What reliable information and controls do I have that give me confidence to make decisions and weather shocks?

Take some time to reflect on what you have learned so far.

Key learnings

1. **The language of business**
   Finance provides stability through accounting, reporting and forecasting, giving leaders visibility and control over performance, cash and risk. Understanding financial statements enables better decision-making.
2. **People and culture as stabilisers**
   Strong HR systems, clear policies, performance management, structured hiring and well-designed rewards create a consistent and trusted environment. Culture and communication foster engagement, accountability and alignment with company goals.
3. **Systems, data and security**
   Reliable IT, strong cybersecurity and intelligent use of data and AI drive efficiency and resilience, enabling smarter, faster decision-making supported by accurate information.

4. **Control, compliance and reputation**
   The legal function protects against unnecessary risk. Contracts, compliance and regulatory discipline prevent costly mistakes, while IP management safeguards innovation.
5. **Clarity and trust through communication**
   Clear, consistent and transparent messaging builds confidence, trust alignment and good reputation.

Final thoughts

For more details and free content on the Stabilise stage, please visit Standardmodelforbusiness.com. Scan the QR code:

Once the foundations have been stabilised, the next challenge is to grow without losing control. That's where the Grow stage begins.

CHAPTER FOUR
Grow

CHAPTER FOUR

Grow

The boardroom was quiet, except for the rhythmic tap of a pen against the table. The CEO leaned forward, eyes fixed on the presentation slide showing a single word in bold: 'scale'.

'This is our moment,' he said. 'We've built a strong foundation, but to lead the market, we'll need to think more like a platform, not a single company or product.'

I was advising the private equity fund that owned a majority stake in the business. The company was profitable, respected and technically competent, but it was fragmented. Each regional subsidiary ran its own systems, suppliers and R&D. The group had potential but no integration or shared direction. It was a classic mid-market scenario: a solid foundation but not a machine for growth.

The fund's investment thesis was straightforward: buy and build. Acquire complementary businesses, consolidate the market, create synergies and build enterprise value. On paper it looked simple; in practice it was a huge amount of coordination across people, products and processes.

The first step was R&D. Each acquisition target had its own research team, developing similar products with small variations for local customers. There was a lot of duplication. The best engineers were brought together from across the group into a central R&D

team. Their mandate was to stop competing and start building together. Within six months, they had designed a modular product platform – one core technology that could be adapted across all markets. What used to take a year to develop now took three months.

Then came partnerships. Scaling organically would have been too slow. The fund needed to move fast, acquiring smaller competitors and suppliers who had niche expertise or loyal customer bases, but the real value wasn't just in buying companies, it was in integrating them effectively. Joint ventures were created with key distributors to open up new markets. Every partnership was evaluated not just for financial return but for fit: culture, systems and long-term synergy.

Logistics became critical to successful growth. The acquisitions had left us with multiple warehouses and transport providers, and incompatible IT systems. Orders got lost between regions and shipping costs reduced profitability. We mapped every flow of material, from supplier to end customer across the entire group, then we redesigned the entire process.

A new centralised logistics hub was built at a major transport crossroads. Outbound logistics were consolidated, warehouse footprints optimised, and a unified inventory system was rolled out across all entities. The savings were clear, but more importantly, the customer experience was transformed. Products arrived faster with fewer errors.

What impressed me most wasn't the financial engineering but the operational integration. True growth didn't come from simply buying more businesses; it came from making them work together. R&D built the future, partnerships opened doors and logistics made it all possible.

In the end, the buy-and-build strategy became more than a financial move, it became part of the culture. A belief that growth is not about speed alone but about synchronisation: aligning innovation, collaboration and execution into one seamless rhythm.

The grow stage is about scaling. Expanding products, services and markets with ambition and discipline. The challenge shifts from survival to sustainable growth. Innovation, collaboration and flawless delivery become the drivers that turn potential into real growth.

The following functions make up the Grow stage: **research & development (R&D)**, **partnerships** and **logistics**.

Research & development

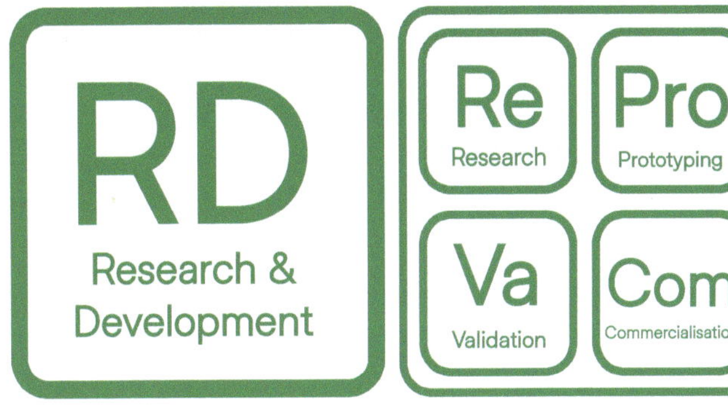

Growth is about creating what's next. R&D drives innovation by improving existing products or services, developing new ones and anticipating customers' ever-evolving needs. R&D transforms ideas into a competitive advantage, ensuring the business does not fall behind the market. Companies that invest in R&D lead and shape their industries.

R&D consists of four interconnected stages: **research, prototyping, validation** and **commercialisation**.

Research

Research is about exploration. Finding ideas, understanding what customers want, what technologies are possible and where the market is heading. It combines data with insight to identify opportunities worth pursuing.

Key elements of research include:

- **Market research.** Analysing customer behaviour, needs and pain points to identify gaps in the market. There needs to be a real problem to solve.
- **Technology.** Understanding emerging technologies, scientific advances or digital tools that can reshape industries. What used to take decades can now happen in months. Being alert to technological shifts is essential.

- **Competitive intelligence.** Understanding what competitors are developing and where they are succeeding. This context allows companies to pursue and position their innovations effectively.
- **Idea generation.** Building structured processes for capturing and reviewing ideas from a dedicated research team, employees, customers and partners. Innovation should not depend on a single visionary, it should be part of the culture.

Research is often misunderstood as blue-sky thinking. In reality, it is about directed curiosity. It is creative exploration guided by significant market research and understanding of what customers need. The best R&D teams are not those that generate the most ideas but those that ask the right questions: What problem are we solving? For whom? How do we solve it?

Prototyping

Prototyping brings ideas to life. It is the rapid movement from an idea to a rough working example of a product or service to visualise and understand what it will look like. Prototyping transforms assumptions into something we can test and improve.

Prototyping consists of:

- **Concept design.** Developing early versions of the product – whether digital mock-ups, 3D models or process simulations – to visualise how the idea works in practice.

- **Rapid iteration.** Building and testing quickly. Prototypes should be rough, fast and disposable. Each iteration provides feedback that shapes the next. The goal is for fast improvement, or to kill a bad idea quickly to minimise development cost.
- **Cross-functional collaboration.** Prototyping is not just for engineers or designers. Coordination across several functions is required, including marketing, finance and operations. Each function brings a different perspective on feasibility, cost and value.
- **Feasibility assessment.** Evaluating whether the idea can be produced at scale, within reasonable cost and time constraints.

Disciplined prototyping encourages experimentation. Failure of a prototype provides further data to improve the next iteration. Companies that prototype well learn faster, spend less and reduce the risk of wasted investment.

Modern tools, from 3D printing to digital twins, have made prototyping faster and more accessible. The underlying principle remains: build, measure, learn.

Validation

Once a prototype is made, it is tested and validated to determine whether the product or service solves a genuine problem and whether customers will pay for it.

Key elements of validation include:

- **Customer validation.** Engaging real users through interviews, focus groups or pilot programmes. Early adopters provide crucial feedback that shapes product design and usability.
- **Market validation.** Running small-scale product launches or tests to measure demand, conversion and price sensitivity.
- **Financial validation.** Modelling the financials: cost of production, expected margins and payback periods, to ensure the concept is commercially viable.
- **Operational validation.** Ensuring the business can support the new product: can it be feasibly produced or sourced? Supply chains, systems and people all need to be ready.

Validation reduces risk before launching a product or service, yet businesses can skip this step, resulting in costly failures.

Effective validation combines qualitative and quantitative insight. Customer feedback explains why something works well or doesn't work, while data from market tests shows how much it matters. Together they allow confident decisions about which products or services to commercialise.

Commercialisation

Commercialisation turns validated ideas into a full product or service. It is the final stage of R&D, where innovation leaves the lab and enters the market.

Key elements of commercialisation include:

- **Go-to-market strategy.** Defining the launch plan: target audience, pricing, distribution channels and messaging. A great product can fail if nobody knows about it or understands its value.
- **Production and supply chain readiness.** Scaling manufacturing or service delivery to meet anticipated demand while maintaining quality and cost efficiency.
- **IP protection.** Registering patents, trademarks or copyrights to protect innovations and maintain a competitive advantage (see the Legal function in the previous chapter).
- **Launch execution and monitoring.** Coordinating marketing, sales and operations to ensure a

smooth rollout. Post-launch, data should be collected on performance and customer response to help inform improvements.

- **Continuous improvement.** Even after launch, products should evolve. Feedback from the market informs R&D for refinements or next-generation designs.

Commercialisation requires close collaboration between R&D and finance, marketing and operations to ensure that the value from innovation is captured by the company.

Partnerships

No business grows in isolation, particularly when it comes to fast growth. Partnerships unlock opportunities, scale, extend reach and reduce risk, open new markets, and bring fresh expertise, whether mergers or acquisitions, suppliers, distributors or strategic allies. The right partnerships amplify the strengths of the business, allowing the company to scale effectively.

Partnerships can be structured into four main categories: **strategic partnerships**, **mergers & acquisitions**, **joint ventures** and **operational partnerships**.

Strategic partnerships

Strategic partnerships are long-term collaborations between two or more organisations that align their strengths for mutual advantage. These are not transactional supplier relationships, they are alliances designed to advance shared goals, such as entering new markets, co-developing products or leveraging each other's distribution and expertise.

Key areas of strategic partnerships are:

- **Strategic alignment.** Both parties must have aligned objectives. If one seeks short-term profit and the other long-term capability, the partnership will not work.
- **Complementary strengths.** Each partner should bring something of value to the partnership, be it technology, customer base, geographic presence or operational excellence. The best partnerships create more value together.

- **Governance and structure.** Scope, decision rights, performance indicators and dispute resolution should be clearly defined in a partnership agreement. Clarity prevents misunderstandings escalating into major issues.
- **Performance measurement.** Partners should track results using agreed metrics: revenue contribution, market share growth, cost savings or innovation milestones. A partnership that cannot be measured cannot be managed.

Strategic partnerships thrive on reciprocity, transparency, open communication and shared wins, which builds trust. They fail when one side dominates or when expectations are misaligned. Regular reviews and renewal discussions keep the relationship purposeful and dynamic.

Mergers & acquisitions

Mergers & acquisitions (M&A) represents the most direct route to growth, buying or merging with another company to gain access to new markets, products or capabilities. When executed well, it accelerates your strategy by years, within months. When executed poorly, it destroys values just as fast. The difference lies in preparation, due diligence and integration discipline.

M&A includes:

- **Strategic fit.** The first question is: Why target this company? An acquisition must clearly fit the long-term direction and strategy, whether expanding customer base, entering new geographies, acquiring technology or achieving economies of scale.
- **Due diligence.** Prior to an acquisition, a comprehensive assessment of financial health, commercials and contracts, operations and legal exposures are essential. Beyond the numbers, cultural compatibility is critical and helps with integration, often determining success.
- **Valuation and deal structure.** A fair price and deal structure should be determined (eg cash, shares, earn-outs) that balances risk and incentives. Overpaying can burden the acquirer for years, reducing the intended value from the deal.
- **Integration planning.** Integration starts before the deal closes. Systems, policies and teams must merge smoothly. The goal is not to impose. This means preserving what works while aligning to common standards.
- **Value creation.** The purpose of any acquisition is to create value. Synergies between the two parties need to be defined and measured post-merger. Many acquisitions fail because of poor integration and lack of value creation.

A successful acquisition feels expansionist; the whole is greater than the sum of its parts. Done right, M&A accelerates a company's strategy by acquiring what it would otherwise have to build, taking a large amount of time and resources. This is easier said than done. Although M&A success has improved over recent decades, it still has a 50:50 chance of success.[19]

Joint ventures

A joint venture (JV) is a legal entity created by two or more parties to pursue a specific opportunity, such as a project or entering a new market or jurisdiction. JVs pool resources, expertise and risk under a jointly owned structure. Unlike strategic partnerships, which are often contractual, JVs create a new legal entity with shared governance, shared risk and shared profits.

Joint ventures can be described as follows:

- **Defined purpose.** A JV must have a clear mission, be it entering a market, developing a technology or delivering a project.
- **Equity and contribution.** Each partner contributes capital, assets, resources or IP and shares profits proportionally. JV agreements specify funding obligations, ownership rights and how new investment will be handled.
- **Governance framework.** JVs establish a board or steering committee with representation from

each partner. Decision-making authority, veto rights and reporting structures should be clearly defined.

- **Exit strategy.** Plan for the end before it begins. Conditions for buyouts, dissolution or monetisation should be agreed by the partners prior to entering into a JV, to avoid a later dispute.
- **Cultural integration.** Even with shared ownership, working practices will be different. A common 'operating language' of shared policies and procedures should be developed.

JVs allow companies to enter high-barrier markets, pool risk and combine technical expertise. They serve as testbeds for experimentation without a full commitment of resources; however, effective JVs require active management and constant communication. When neglected, JVs become bureaucratic and slow; when nurtured, they create a competitive advantage.

Operational partnerships

Operational partnerships are tactical collaborations that strengthen daily execution. For example, co-manufacturing, outsourcing, shared logistics networks or technology service agreements. They expand capability and capacity without increasing headcount or fixed cost, allowing the company to remain agile while scaling. Many partnerships offer pay-as-you-go services and pricing structures, eg cloud computing.

Areas of operational partnerships include:

- **Vendor selection.** Choosing the right partners through a transparent procurement process and objective evaluation of bidders. Reliability, quality and cultural fit are just as important as cost.
- **SLAs.** Clearly defined performance metrics, such as delivery times, uptime or defect rates, ensure accountability of the partner. SLAs create trust between partners.
- **Process interfacing.** The interface between partners, data and workflow should be fully integrated and seamless. Automation and shared dashboards improve visibility and control.
- **Cost and risk management.** Outsourcing to low-cost jurisdictions helps to manage cost but introduces new risks. Oversight, contingency planning and contractual safeguards are essential.
- **Continuous improvement.** Operational partnerships should have a continuous improvement mindset. Periodic reviews of performance, pricing and innovation keep the partnership effective and productive.

Operational partnerships create efficiency and resilience, allowing companies to focus on their core competencies while leveraging their partners for specialist expertise, facilitating growth.

Logistics

As a business scales, delivering products or services quickly becomes key. Efficient logistics ensures products, services and resources flow smoothly from creation to customer, which is only visible when it fails.

In the Grow stage, logistics evolves into a strategic capability, designing efficient and stable systems that enable scale, efficiency and customer satisfaction. The focus shifts from simply fulfilling orders to optimising the entire supply chain.

Logistics comprises four key units: **inbound & outbound logistics**, **returns management**, **warehousing & internal logistics** and **distribution**.

Inbound & outbound logistics

Inbound & outbound logistics are the twin arteries of the supply chain. Inbound logistics focuses on how raw materials, components and supplies enter the business; outbound logistics ensures finished goods reach customers on time and in perfect condition.

Inbound logistics covers sourcing, transportation and handling of all materials required for production. Its effectiveness determines production continuity and cost efficiency.

Key responsibilities include:

- **Supplier management.** Selecting and managing reliable suppliers to ensure consistent quality and timely delivery.
- **Procurement coordination.** Aligning purchasing schedules and lead times with production plans to minimise excess inventory and shortages.
- **Transportation and receiving.** Choosing optimal routes, carriers and shipping modes to balance speed, cost and sustainability.
- **Inspection and quality control.** Ensuring that raw materials or components received are of high quality, and quantity and type are as ordered.
- **Inventory placement.** Monitoring incoming stock to efficiently store within the warehouse.

Outbound logistics covers everything from packaging and shipping to final delivery. The effectiveness of outbound logistics defines the customer experience.

Key responsibilities include:

- **Order fulfilment.** Ensuring that customer orders are processed accurately, packed securely and dispatched on time.
- **Delivery optimisation.** Planning transport routes, type of transport (land, sea or air) and schedules for cost-effective, reliable deliveries.
- **Customer communication.** Providing real-time tracking and proactive updates to manage customer expectations and increase transparency of the delivery process.
- **Performance measurement.** Tracking on-time delivery rates, fulfilment accuracy and transportation costs.

When inbound and outbound logistics are aligned, operations flow smoothly. Suppliers deliver on time, production runs uninterrupted and customers receive goods when promised. Misalignment causes costly delays, stock-outs or overstocking, impacting profits and reputation with customers.

Returns management

Returns are unavoidable. How your company handles returns reveals its operational maturity and mindset towards customers. Returns management focuses on mastering the return of goods, information and refunds.

Returns management can be described by the following:

- **Reverse logistics.** Designing systems for product returns, repairs, replacements or recycling. This includes setting up dedicated return channels or automated returns authorisation systems.
- **Quality assessment.** Inspecting returned goods to determine whether they can be resold, refurbished or scrapped.
- **Root cause analysis.** Analysing data to identify why returns occur. This could be due to faulty products, packaging issues, unclear instructions or logistical errors. Identifying the root cause and addressing the lessons learned should reduce future returns and costs.
- **Customer resolution.** Handling refunds, credits or replacements promptly and transparently to maintain a high level of trust. (See Customer service centre in Chapter 2.)

An efficient returns process enhances the customer experience and builds trust. An easy returns policy is often a deciding factor in purchasing decisions. Effective returns management can convert potential customer dissatisfaction into loyalty.

Warehousing & internal logistics

Warehousing and internal logistics are the 'behind the scenes' of a company's operations. They connect production, inventory and distribution, ensuring goods are stored safely, handled efficiently and moved precisely where and when needed.

Key responsibilities include:

- **Warehouse layout and design.** Planning optimal storage configurations to reduce handling time and maximise space utilisation increases efficiency. This includes zoning areas for receiving, storage, picking, packing and dispatch.
- **Inventory management.** Monitoring stock levels to balance supply and demand. Too much inventory ties up capital and increases storage costs; too little disrupts sales and production.
- **Automation and technology.** Using warehouse management systems, barcoding, robotics and tracking to increase 'uptime' of the warehouse and enhance accuracy and speed.

- **Safety and compliance.** Implementing standards for equipment, fire safety and employee welfare in line with health regulations.
- **Internal movement.** Coordinating the flow of materials between departments, plants or production lines to ensure seamless operations and avoid bottlenecks.

As businesses scale, warehouse strategy becomes a competitive differentiator. Whether through automation, strategic location or design efficiency, high-performing warehousing reduces lead times, increases throughput and strengthens resilience against supply chain shocks.

Distribution

Distribution determines how effectively products reach their destinations and how efficiently the company converts production into revenue. In many industries, distribution is the decisive factor that differentiates leaders from laggards.[20]

Key areas include:

- **Distribution channel strategy.** Defining the mix of direct, retail, wholesale and online distribution channels to reach target markets effectively. Each has different cost structures, margins and risks.

- **Network design.** Selecting locations for distribution centres and hubs to balance proximity to customers with operational efficiency.
- **Transportation management.** Negotiating carrier contracts, managing fleet operations and optimising delivery schedules.
- **Performance metrics.** Tracking delivery times, cost per shipment, fulfilment rates and customer satisfaction scores.
- **Scalability.** Ensuring the distribution network can handle growth without sacrificing service quality.

With international expansion, distribution becomes more complex. Global trade requires navigating customs, tariffs, local regulations and cross-border shipping challenges. Strategic partnerships with global logistics providers can help manage this complexity while maintaining service levels.

QUESTIONS FOR YOU

1. How does your company currently generate, validate and commercialise new ideas?
2. Which partnerships could effectively multiply your growth?
3. How does your logistics system currently affect your business, in terms of both cost and reputation? Where does it create competitive advantage, if at all?

Take some time to reflect on what you have learned so far.

Key learnings

1. **Innovation drives sustained growth**
   R&D transforms curiosity into a competitive advantage through structured experimentation and disciplined validation.
2. **Partnerships multiply capacity**
   Collaboration expands reach, reduces risk and accelerates scale beyond what's possible alone.
3. **Execution determines success**
   Growth depends on operational excellence: logistics, delivery and customer fulfilment done at scale.
4. **Integration sustains growth**
   The flow from idea to partnership to delivery must be seamless; weak links slow momentum.
5. **Growth introduces complexity**
   Managing that complexity prepares the business for the next stage: governance and control.

Final thoughts

For more details and free content on the Grow stage, please visit Standardmodelforbusiness.com. Scan the QR code:

As growth accelerates, so does complexity and the need for stronger governance. The next stage, Govern, describes just that.

CHAPTER FIVE
Govern

CHAPTER FIVE
Govern

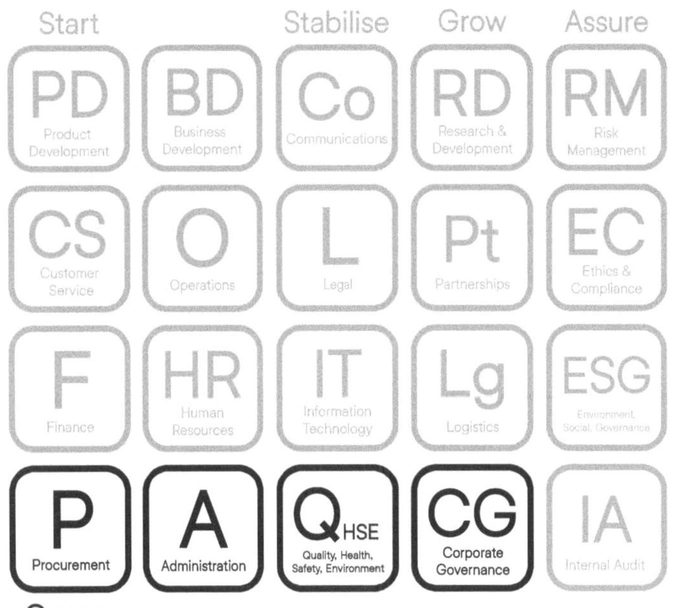

The armed police officer shouted, 'Laptops out of bags!' to the people filtering through the x-ray security gates. He wore a thick, black bulletproof vest. A machine gun hung from a strap around his neck.

As I walked through the metal detector and collected my belongings, I tried to reconcile the grandeur of my surroundings with the necessity of such intense security. The entrance hall was magnificent. Gothic arches stretched skyward; the stonework carried the weight of government. I was entering the Houses of Parliament in London.

The interior was confusing to navigate. It was evening. The lighting was dim. In the shadows, I saw people in one-to-one conversations or gathered in small groups. I imagined they were plotting and scheming to advance their political careers, and for the good of the country. Yes, in that order.

I asked a member of staff for directions to the bar where I was to meet the Baroness, who was on the board of a National Health Trust I was auditing in Westminster.

She spoke with confidence, born of years in public service: 'Governance isn't just paperwork, Mr. Rowe. It's the architecture of accountability.' That line stayed with me.

Her role was to oversee finance and risk, and also how the Trust managed procurement, administration and quality – areas that were too often seen as operational but were central to governance.

'Procurement,' she explained, 'isn't only about getting the best price, it's about supply chain integrity. How you buy reflects your ethics. How you choose suppliers reflects your values. Corruption doesn't begin with envelopes; it begins with convenience.'

Every tender, every supplier decision, every conflict of interest. These were the real tests of governance, not the minutes of a board meeting.

'Administration,' she continued, 'is the silent engine. Policies, records, meeting minutes, decision logs. They keep an organisation coherent, transparent. Without them, memory fades, accountability blurs and chaos sets in. You can't run a hospital, or a government, without good administrators.'

We turned to QHSE; quality, health, safety and environment. 'People think of it as compliance,' she said, 'but it's culture, especially in healthcare. If people cut corners on safety, they'll cut corners everywhere.'

This resonated deeply. Governance was not abstract, it was lived through daily discipline, standards and the courage to stop when something feels wrong.

'Corporate governance,' she said, 'isn't a department. It's the conscience of the organisation. It's how we behave when no one is watching.'

The board's duty, she reminded me, was not to manage but to ensure management was sound; to question, to guide, to safeguard the long-term viability of the organisation. 'We are,' she said, 'custodians of trust.'

'The strongest boards,' she continued, 'are the ones that ask the right questions at the right time.'

As our meeting ended, I realised governance was not just a set of committees, documents or code. It was a mindset. It was culture. It was the tone from the top.

As I left the Houses of Parliament I thought: Governance is invisible when it works, but everything can fall apart when it doesn't.

The Govern stage is where discipline and oversight protect the business. It introduces the structures and safeguards that keep performance high, risks under control and stakeholders confident in the company's direction.

Good governance ensures cohesiveness across the business. As your company grows to over 100 people, it becomes harder to manage and ensure a consistent corporate culture. The word 'siloed' is common here.

Four functions support the Govern stage: **procurement, administration, quality, health, safety & environment (QHSE)** and **corporate governance**.

Procurement

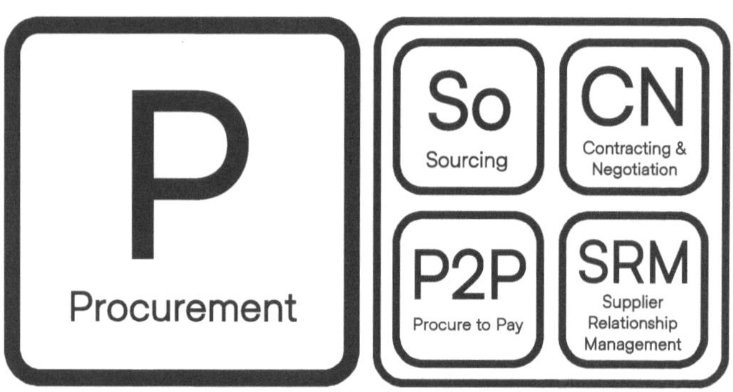

Procurement is more than just buying; it is securing the right resources at the right time for the right price. A strong procurement function creates resilience in supply chains, reduces costs and ensures quality inputs. Choices about suppliers can make or break long-term performance. Done well, procurement shifts from a transactional activity to a competitive advantage.

Procurement can be divided into four key areas: **sourcing, contracting & negotiation, procure to pay** and **supplier relationship management**. Together, they ensure spending is efficient, transparent and aligned with business objectives.

Sourcing

Sourcing is the process of identifying, evaluating and selecting suppliers to meet the needs of the business. The goal is to achieve the best balance between cost, quality, reliability and sustainability.

Sourcing follows a structured approach:

- **Market analysis.** Understanding the supply market, trends and risks to identify the best opportunities for supply value.
- **Specification.** Clearly defining what is needed, ensuring requirements are not over-engineered and focusing on total cost rather than just initial price.
- **Supplier selection.** Conducting competitive bidding through requests for quotation (RFQs) or requests for proposal (RFPs) and evaluating suppliers on technical quality and commercials.
- **Evaluation and award.** Using a fair and transparent evaluation process, often with weighted scoring, to ensure procurement decisions are evidence-based and auditable.

Effective sourcing aims to build long-term supply stability and performance rather than short-term savings. Ethical and transparent sourcing practices are essential, ensuring compliance with anti-bribery and conflict-of-interest regulations. In large companies, even small improvements in sourcing can translate into significant savings over the long term, and improved control over supply risk and supplier performance.

Contracting & negotiation

Once suppliers have been selected, a contract needs to be negotiated. This formalises the relationship between supplier and buyer, defining rights, obligations and performance expectations for both parties. A strong contract turns intent into an enforceable agreement.

Contracting ensures that the agreement is clear, consistent and compliant. Standard contract templates help maintain consistency and reduce legal risk. Every contract should include key elements such as:

- **Scope of work.** Details about what is being purchased, with clear deliverables and specifications.
- **Commercial terms.** Agreed pricing, payment terms and duration of the contract.
- **Performance requirements.** KPIs or SLAs that measure quality, fulfilment and responsiveness.
- **Risk allocation.** Defining responsibility for potential risks such as delays, defects, data breaches or regulatory non-compliance.

- **Termination and renewal.** Outlining exit rights and renewal processes to avoid unplanned extensions or supplier dependency.

Negotiating contract terms is where value is captured for both parties. Effective negotiation aims for win-win outcomes that balance price with value and develops a long-term mutually beneficial partnership. Negotiating should create sustainable value, not simply drive costs down. Successful negotiators prepare a clear strategy – what they need and what concessions they can make – while maintaining integrity and professionalism throughout the contracting process.

Procure to pay

Procure to pay (P2P) is the end-to-end process of purchasing from initial request to supplier payment. It ensures that spending is authorised, transparent and compliant. A disciplined P2P process reduces waste, prevents fraud and gives leaders visibility into where the company's money is going.

The P2P cycle includes:

- **Requisition.** A purchase request is raised for goods or services and approved by the correct authority, different to the requisition raiser.
- **Purchase order (PO).** A PO is created and approved, specifying the product or service, quantity, price and delivery terms.

- **Receipt.** Once the goods or services are delivered, goods are inspected and both goods and services are confirmed as received.
- **Invoice.** The supplier submits an invoice for the goods or service, in which all details are matched to the PO and receipt.
- **Payment.** The invoice is approved and paid according to the agreed payment terms (eg within 30 days after invoice).

Modern P2P IT systems, often integrated within ERP systems, automate this workflow. Automation reduces errors, ensures three-way matching (PO, receipt and invoice), and provides real-time data on spending patterns and supplier performance.

Critical here is a segregation of duties, which ensures that no single person can initiate, approve and pay for a transaction.

An effective P2P process provides transparency and predictability. It allows finance teams to forecast cash flow accurately, ensures suppliers are paid on time and provides management with a complete view of committed and actual spending.

Supplier relationship management

Once contracts are signed and suppliers are onboarded, supplier relationship management (SRM) ensures ongoing performance, value and collaboration between the company and its suppliers. SRM is the process of managing suppliers to meet contractual obligations, drive improvement and reduce risk.

Key elements of SRM include:

- **Performance management.** Monitoring supplier KPIs, delivery times, quality levels and responsiveness. Regular supplier reviews ensure accountability and continuous improvement.
- **Collaboration and innovation.** Engaging strategic suppliers in joint problem-solving, cost reduction and product or service innovation. Many breakthrough improvements originate from supplier expertise.
- **Risk management.** Assessing and monitoring supplier financial stability, operational capacity and compliance with environmental and ethical standards. Diversifying the supplier base reduces dependency and ensures resilience.
- **Sustainability and ESG.** Evaluating suppliers' environmental and social impact. Ethical sourcing, labour practices, and carbon-reduction commitments are increasingly central to brand reputation.
- **Segmentation.** Distinguishing between strategic, preferred and transactional suppliers ensures that attention and resources are focused where they deliver the most value.

Strong supplier relationships are built on transparency, fairness and shared goals. When managed effectively, SRM transforms procurement from a cost-control function into a value-creation engine. It builds resilience across the supply chain and positions procurement as a strategic contributor to growth, innovation and trust.

Procurement, when governed effectively, ensures that every dollar spent is purposeful, controlled and aligned with strategy. It transforms spending from an operational necessity into a disciplined process that drives efficiency, resilience and integrity across the entire business.

Administration

Administration is the behind-the-scenes infrastructure that keeps a company running smoothly. It covers the systems and processes that free people to focus on value creation instead of firefighting. Effective admin provides clarity to employees, saves time and ensures consistency, helping to build a platform for scale and control.

Administration can be divided into four key areas: **office management**, **documents & records management**, **employee & executive support**, and **facilities & services**. Each plays a vital role in ensuring the company operates efficiently, reliably and professionally.

Office management

Office management provides structure to the day-to-day environment in which people work. It covers the coordination of resources, logistics and operational processes that keep the business functioning efficiently. A well-managed office creates an atmosphere of order and professionalism, supporting productivity and morale across all teams.

Key responsibilities include:

- **Operational coordination.** Managing office supplies, stationery, meeting rooms, travel logistics and communications.
- **Administrative procedures.** Defining and standardising procedures for approvals, correspondence, mail, visitor management and other recurring tasks. Standardisation reduces

errors and ensures consistency across offices and regions.

- **Budget and procurement alignment.** Managing departmental budgets, approving small purchases within delegated authority and ensuring alignment with the procurement function for larger spend.
- **Health, safety & environment (HSE) compliance.** Ensuring that the physical workspace meets safety, accessibility and ergonomic standards. Regular inspections, maintenance schedules and compliance logs protect both employees and the company from unnecessary risk.
- **Technology and equipment.** Coordinating with IT for the provisioning of laptops, printers and communications systems, ensuring that staff have the tools needed to perform effectively.

Documents & records management

Documents and records help preserve corporate memory. They contain the evidence of decisions made, transactions completed and obligations accepted, ensuring transparency to all stakeholders, both internal and external to the company. Managing documents and records effectively protects the company's interests and ensures compliance.

Documents & records management involves controlling the entire life cycle of records, from creation and storage to retrieval and disposal. The aim is to ensure that information is accurate, accessible and secure throughout its useful life.

An effective process includes:

- **Classification and control.** Establishing a standard taxonomy and filing structure across the organisation, whether digital or physical (or both). This avoids duplication, confusion or loss of important information.
- **Access and security.** Defining permissions and controls to ensure that only authorised individuals can access sensitive information. Confidential records such as contracts, HR files or financial statements must be stored securely and handled in compliance with data protection laws.
- **Retention and disposal.** Implementing a records retention schedule that defines how long each type of document must be kept. This ensures compliance with regulatory requirements while avoiding unnecessary storage costs.
- **Digital transformation.** Increasingly, companies are moving from paper-based systems to digital. Document management systems and cloud repositories enable version control, audit trails

and searchability, reducing cost, administrative effort and error.

- **Legal and audit readiness.** Well-managed records support internal and external audits, legal proceedings and regulatory reviews. Being able to retrieve accurate documentation quickly signals strong governance.

Poor records management creates significant risk. Missing contracts, outdated policies or lost approvals exposes the company to financial loss, compliance breaches or reputational damage. Strong document and records management provides a foundation of traceability, integrity and trust, signalling to stakeholders that we take business seriously.

Employee & executive support

Employee & executive support ensures that people across the business, from entry-level staff to senior leadership, have the logistical and administrative assistance needed to perform at their best.

Employee support focuses on helping staff navigate internal processes efficiently. This includes coordinating onboarding logistics, scheduling training, arranging travel, managing internal communications and supporting company events or meetings. Administrative staff are often the first point of contact for many employees and play a key role in shaping the company's internal culture of professionalism and support.

Executive support serves the leadership team directly. Executive assistants (EAs) and chiefs of staff coordinate schedules, manage correspondence, prepare presentations and reports, and ensure leaders have the information they need to make timely decisions. They act as a central hub, connecting departments and maintaining flow between strategic direction and operational execution.

Key responsibilities in this area include:

- **Scheduling and coordination.** Managing calendars, meetings and travel logistics, ensuring time is used efficiently and priorities are met.
- **Information preparation.** Drafting reports, presentations or summaries that provide leadership with clear, actionable information.
- **Confidentiality and discretion.** Handling sensitive matters with integrity and always maintaining trust.
- **Communication flow.** Acting as a bridge between executives and teams, ensuring that messages, instructions and follow-ups are consistent and timely.

High-performing administrative professionals increase overall productivity and efficiency, allowing others to focus on revenue-generating activities. They cut through complexity to provide clarity over office operations.

Facilities & services

Facilities & services manages the physical and logistical infrastructure that supports daily operations. It ensures that workplaces are safe, efficient and fit for purpose. Facilities teams manage everything from office leases to cleaning contracts, catering, security and maintenance.

Key areas include:

- **Space planning.** Ensuring that office layouts support collaboration, efficiency and safety. This includes managing moves, expansions and workspace redesigns.
- **Maintenance and asset management.** Keeping buildings, systems and equipment in working order through preventive maintenance schedules and asset tracking.
- **Service contracts.** Overseeing suppliers such as security, cleaning, catering and waste management. Each service is managed through clearly defined contracts and performance standards.

- **Sustainability.** Implementing environmentally responsible practices such as energy efficiency, recycling programmes and carbon tracking. Facilities management plays a growing role in achieving corporate sustainability goals.
- **Business continuity.** Facilities must be part of the company's continuity planning. Backup sites, generator power, emergency procedures and evacuation plans ensure resilience during disruptions.

Effective facilities & services creates an environment that reflects the company's values: professional, safe and sustainable. It directly impacts employee satisfaction, productivity and brand image.

Quality, health, safety & environment

Quality, health, safety & environment (QHSE) protects people, safeguards the environment and ensures regulations are consistently met. It reflects the values of a business and its commitment to do the right thing. A key part of reputation management, QHSE performed well helps to protect your company, building trust with stakeholders and reducing risk.

QHSE can be divided into four interconnected areas: **quality management**, **health & safety management**, **environmental management**, and **management systems & certification**.

Quality management

Quality management ensures that the company consistently delivers products and services that meet and surpass customer requirements and regulatory standards. It is not simply about inspection or control; it is about building quality into every process, decision and behaviour.

Quality management includes the following:

- **Process control.** Defining clear procedures, roles and responsibilities to ensure consistent output. Standard operating procedures (SOPs) form the backbone of process discipline.
- **Monitoring and measurement.** Using KPIs such as defect rates, customer complaints and rework levels to measure performance and identify trends.

- **Corrective and preventive actions.** Investigating the root cause of non-conformances and implementing solutions that prevent recurrence.
- **Quality audits and quality reviews.** Conducting regular reviews to verify compliance with quality standards and to identify improvement opportunities.
- **Customer feedback.** Integrating feedback loops to refine products and services continuously, ensuring that customer feedback drives improvement.
- **Quality systems.** A quality system may be implemented to ensure consistency in production. Significant planning and discipline are required to implement and maintain a quality system, but the benefits are significant: fewer customer returns, smoother sales processes and better customer feedback and retention.

Quality is not the responsibility of a single department; it is a collective mindset. Companies with mature quality management systems cultivate a culture where everyone, from front-line staff to leadership, takes ownership of doing things right first time.

Health & safety management

Health & safety management protects the wellbeing of employees, contractors and visitors. It ensures that every person goes home in the same or a better condition than they arrived. Safety is not only a legal obligation, it is a moral one.

A strong safety culture starts with commitment from leadership. Senior management must visibly champion safety, allocate resources and model the behaviours expected of others.

Key elements of an effective health & safety system include:

- **Hazard identification and risk assessment.** Systematically identifying workplace hazards and assessing associated risks to determine appropriate controls.
- **Policies and procedures.** Establishing clear rules for incident reporting, emergency response, personal protective equipment and safe working practices.
- **Training and competence.** Ensuring employees are trained and competent for the tasks they perform. Refresher training and awareness campaigns keep safety top of mind.
- **Incident management.** Recording, investigating and learning from accidents, near misses and unsafe conditions. Lessons learned should feed directly into preventive measures.

- **Health and wellbeing.** Expanding beyond physical safety to include mental health, ergonomics and occupational health monitoring.

Leading companies build a safety culture where people feel safe to speak up, stop unsafe work and report issues without fear. The aim is to move from compliance-based to behaviour-based safety, where doing the right thing becomes second nature.

Environmental management

Environmental management ensures that the company operates responsibly and sustainably. It minimises negative impacts on the natural environment while aligning operations with the principles of efficiency and stewardship. Increasingly, stakeholders expect companies to demonstrate measurable environmental performance.

An effective environmental management framework focuses on three key goals: compliance, efficiency and sustainability.

Core components include:

- **Environmental policy.** A statement of commitment to reduce environmental impact and meet or exceed regulatory standards.

- **Impact assessment.** Identifying and evaluating environmental aspects of operations, such as energy consumption, waste generation, emissions and resource use.
- **Targets and programmes.** Setting measurable objectives such as carbon reduction, water conservation or waste diversion, and establishing initiatives to achieve them.
- **Pollution prevention and waste management.** Implementing practices to minimise waste, reuse materials and reduce emissions to air, land and water.
- **Sustainability reporting.** Monitoring performance against environmental KPIs and communicating progress transparently to stakeholders.

Environmental management is also about efficiency and innovation. Reducing waste and energy use lowers costs, increases profits, enhances brand reputation and prepares the business for emerging regulatory and investor expectations, ultimately raising the value of the company. It pays to be green.[21]

Management systems & certification

Management systems provide the structured framework through which QHSE operates. They ensure consistency, accountability and continual improvement across the business. The International Organization for Standardization (ISO)[22] issues SOPs for companies to demonstrate to stakeholders that they take these areas seriously and have the discipline to implement. These processes are audited and certified.

Common frameworks include:

- **ISO 9001** – Quality management systems.[23]
- **ISO 45001** – Occupational health & safety management.[24]
- **ISO 14001** – Environmental management systems.[25]
- **ISO 50001** – Energy management systems.[26]

Each standard follows the plan–do–check–act cycle,[27] promoting continuous improvement:

1. **Plan.** Establish objectives and processes.
2. **Do.** Implement the processes.
3. **Check.** Monitor and measure results.
4. **Act.** Take corrective actions to improve performance.

Certification provides an independent seal of credibility that strengthens customer confidence, supports tenders and demonstrates compliance to regulators and investors. It also drives internal efficiency through clear documentation, defined accountability and structured performance reviews.

Management systems also embed QHSE into the company's culture. They create clarity on how things should be done, why they should be done that way and how improvement is measured.

QHSE ensures that the business operates with integrity, care and discipline. It safeguards people, protects the environment and assures customers that quality and safety are never compromised.

Corporate governance

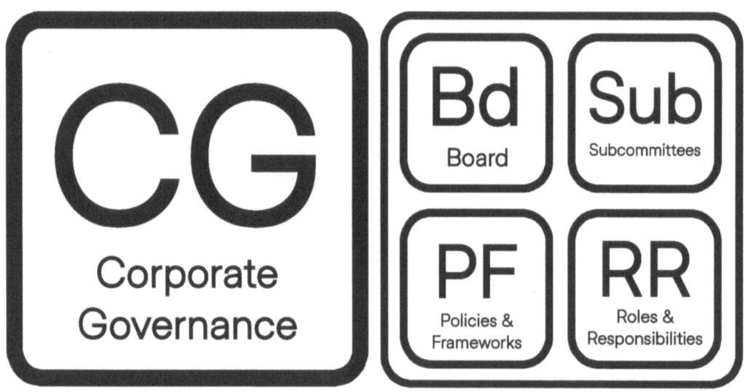

Corporate governance is the framework that aligns leadership decisions with stakeholder expectations. Boards, policies and oversight structures increase accountability and transparency, ensuring the business is run responsibly. Good governance strengthens decision-making, protects reputation and ensures growth is sustainable. It builds trust between the business and its stakeholders.

Corporate governance can be described by four key areas: **board, subcommittees, policies & frameworks** and **roles & responsibilities**.

Board

The board of directors is responsible for the overall direction, performance and stewardship of the company. The board represents the interests of shareholders but must also balance those interests with those of employees, customers, regulators and wider stakeholders.

An effective board operates on three core principles: independence, competence and accountability. Key considerations for the board are:

- **Composition.** A well-structured board combines executive directors (who are responsible for the business) and non-executive directors (who provide independent oversight and challenge). Diversity in experience, background and perspective enhances decision quality and reduces the risk of groupthink.
- **Responsibilities.** The board approves strategy and budgets, oversees major investments and ensures the company operates within legal and

ethical boundaries. It is also responsible for appointing and evaluating the CEO, ensuring succession planning for senior leadership and safeguarding the integrity of financial reporting.

- **Governance conduct.** The chair leads the board, ensuring meetings are well-structured, debate is balanced and decisions are documented. The company secretary supports the chair and board in compliance, record keeping and corporate filings. Together, they maintain the formality and transparency that underpin trust in governance.
- **Board dynamics.** Strong boards foster constructive tension, open discussion and challenge, without hostility. The goal is collective decision-making informed by diverse viewpoints. Often conducted annually, board evaluations assess performance and identify areas for improvement.

A capable board provides clear leadership. It asks the right questions, holds management accountable and aligned with shareholders, and ensures the company delivers long-term value, ethically and sustainably.

Subcommittees

Board subcommittees provide deeper oversight of critical areas of governance. They enable focused attention on complex or high-risk matters while ensuring transparency and accountability to the full board. Board members form subcommittees to deep dive on certain subjects that the main board may not have time to do.

The main subcommittees include:

- **Audit, risk and compliance committee.** Oversees the financial audit, internal controls, risk management and compliance. It liaises closely with internal and external auditors, reviews audit findings and ensures that management implements recommendations. Some companies have separate committees for audit, risk or compliance, depending on the workload and industry.
- **Remuneration committee.** Defines executive pay and incentive structures, ensuring alignment between performance, reward and shareholder value. It also considers fairness and transparency across the wider workforce.
- **Nomination and governance committee.** Manages board composition, succession planning and the evaluation of directors. It also ensures governance policies remain current and effective.

Each committee operates under a formal charter defining its scope, authority and reporting obligations. Meetings are documented, actions tracked and results reported back to the full board for review.

Effective committees do not operate in isolation; they act as extensions of the board's oversight. Their strength lies in detailed scrutiny, ensuring that no area of governance escapes visibility or accountability.

Policies & frameworks

Policies & frameworks translate governance principles into reality. They set the boundaries within which decisions are made, ensuring consistency, compliance and integrity across the company.

Policies define standards for behaviour, conduct and decision-making. Core governance policies include:

- Delegation of authority
- Code of conduct and ethics
- Conflicts of interest
- Anti-bribery and corruption
- Whistleblowing
- Risk management
- Financial reporting
- Treasury
- HR/people
- IT security
- Investment & capital

Each policy provides clarity on what is expected, who is responsible and what happens if rules are breached.

Frameworks provide structure to how governance operates in practice. Key examples include:

- **Risk management framework.** Defines how risks are identified, assessed, mitigated and monitored.
- **Internal control framework.** Outlines systems and checks that prevent error or fraud and ensure reliability of reporting.
- **Compliance framework.** Ensures adherence to laws, regulations and standards in every jurisdiction of operation.
- **Decision-making framework.** Clarifies which decisions require board approval, which can be delegated and which must be escalated.

Together, policies and frameworks provide the required discipline for good governance. They embed structure, accountability and ethical standards into daily operations.

Governance policies & frameworks should be regularly reviewed and updated to reflect regulatory change, organisational growth and lessons learned from internal or external events.

Roles & responsibilities

Good governance depends on the clarity of roles & responsibilities. Everyone in the company – from the board to front-line staff – plays a part in upholding it. Roles & responsibilities include:

- **Board and management.** The board sets direction; management executes it. The board's role is oversight, not operation – it asks what and why; management focuses on how. This separation ensures accountability and prevents concentration of power.
- **CEO.** The CEO is the bridge between the board and the business, translating strategic objectives into operational plans and ensuring that governance principles are embedded into execution.
- **Executives and senior leaders.** These roles implement governance frameworks within their functions, ensuring policies, controls and reporting are applied consistently. They are accountable for compliance, performance and ethical leadership.
- **Employees.** The employees uphold policies in daily behaviour, raise concerns when standards are breached and contribute to a culture of responsibility.

Clear accountability lines prevent duplication, confusion and gaps in oversight. When everyone knows their role, governance becomes natural, not bureaucratic.

Corporate governance is the foundation of trust. It provides the discipline and transparency that underpin long-term success.

QUESTIONS FOR YOU

1. How do your systems of procurement, administration and quality create transparency and control?
2. If governance is the conscience of the company, how clearly can you define who the true custodians of trust are in your business today?

Take some time to reflect on what you have learned so far.

Key learnings

1. **Governance is culture, not paperwork**
   It lives in daily behaviour, decision-making and the tone set from the top, not in policies or committees alone.

2. **Procurement reflects corporate ethics**
   Every supplier choice and contract negotiation signals a company's integrity, shaping its resilience, reputation and long-term value.

3. **Administration preserves organisational memory**
   Strong records, clear procedures and disciplined documentation protect accountability and prevent chaos as the business grows.

4. **QHSE is the measure of care**
   A company that takes quality, safety and the environment seriously builds trust with employees, customers and society, reducing risk while enhancing reputation.

5. **Corporate governance is the architecture of accountability**
   Clear roles, independent oversight and ethical leadership create transparency, safeguard value and ensure the business endures.

Final thoughts

For more details and free content on the Govern stage, please visit Standardmodelforbusiness.com. Scan the QR code:

With strong governance in place, the final step is to build lasting confidence, not only within the business but also with investors, regulators and the public. The Assure stage focuses on transparency, accountability and trust, ensuring that what has been built can stand up to scrutiny and endure over time.

CHAPTER SIX

Assure

CHAPTER SIX

Assure

As a graduate trainee at Grant Thornton, I learned how people, pressure and imperfect processes make business work. I learned about assurance: frameworks, controls, risk registers and the discipline of asking questions until the real picture emerged.

Later at KPMG, working within the Audit Committee Institute, I advised board members on their responsibilities, governance structures and risk oversight. Here I first encountered the tension at the heart of assurance: leaders want clarity but the world offers complexity. I helped bridge that gap. I saw how governance shapes decision-making, culture and ultimately performance. It planted the seed for my long-standing focus on strengthening businesses from the inside out.

My first leadership role came when I became Group Assurance Manager at a distribution company operating across Western Europe. I built an audit function to provide assurance over risks. I designed audit plans, developed policies and procedures, challenged operations and saw how small governance failures could ripple across an entire business. It taught me the value of simplicity, clarity and relentless follow-through. Assurance mattered because it protected people, performance and reputation.

In 2010, I moved to Abu Dhabi and joined a sovereign wealth fund unlike anything I had experienced before. Over the next fifteen years, my work spanned sectors from aerospace to renewables, advanced manufacturing to IT and communications, and healthcare to global investment platforms. I saw how assurance operates when billions of dollars are at stake and the pace of transformation never slows.

Internal audit became my foundation. I managed and led assurance over portfolios worth billions, delivered large-scale audit plans and worked closely with investment teams to understand how strategy, risk and execution intersected on the ground. I travelled the world meeting teams, looking at companies, reviewing operations and gathering the one thing assurance thrives on: fact-based, objective truth. I learned not just to assess a control environment but to read a room, challenge without confrontation and build trust in the moments when it mattered most.

As Head of Internal Audit Operations, I helped manage a team of over forty professionals. I ran the risk assessment process, built audit plans, managed the budget, improved methodology, supported audit committee reporting and shaped the function through multiple phases of evolution. This was governance at scale, designing how processes should work across a global investment powerhouse.

Risk management became central; I saw how it is a way of thinking. It guides investment decisions, shapes portfolio strategy and acts as the counterbalance to unchecked ambition. I helped embed this mindset into planning cycles, investment discussions and oversight structures. The more senior the conversation, the more risk and strategy became inseparable.

Ethics and compliance always featured throughout my career. Working closely with audit committees and leadership teams, I advised on governance, compliance culture and investigations and provided oversight. I saw the consequences of drifting values, and the strength gained by upholding them. Ethics is a choice. Compliance provides clarity. Together, they act as the moral compass of a company.

My years advising the audit, risk and compliance committee of a large sustainability company in Abu Dhabi were another defining chapter of my career. The company operates at the centre of the clean-energy revolution, and the challenges were global, complex and deeply interconnected. ESG became a strategic imperative. Environmental impact, social responsibility and governance structures shape investor confidence, influence partnerships and determine long-term performance. ESG is a new lens through which businesses are judged.

In 2024, I stepped into my current role building the internal audit and risk management functions for a sovereign private equity firm in Abu Dhabi, with over $400 billion in assets under management. The responsibility is significant: to establish functions that provide independent assurance across one of the most dynamic investment platforms in the world.

Across twenty-one years, the four pillars of Assure have shaped both my career and my world view. Assurance sits at the final stage of The Standard Model for Business for a reason: it is where ambition meets accountability. It ensures that decisions stand up to scrutiny, that values are upheld under pressure and that companies can grow without compromising integrity. It has been my world for a long time, and the lessons it has taught me form the foundation of this chapter.

The final stage of The Standard Model for Business is Assure. Companies rely on assurance functions to address the agency problem; the potential conflict of interest between principals (shareholders) and agents (senior management). Assurance provides transparency, accountability and confidence that the business is being run responsibly, not just efficiently.

There are four functions that support the Assure stage: **risk management**, **ethics & compliance (E&C)**, **environment, social, governance (ESG)** and **internal audit**.

Risk management

Risk management attempts to peer into the future. It is a realm of possibilities and probability, of uncertainty, and it is challenging because people prefer certainty. Risk management identifies threats before they materialise and prepares responses that protect the business. It balances ambition with caution, enabling CEOs to confidently take bold moves. A strong risk function prevents or reduces loss while enabling well-informed decisions, building resilience for the unexpected.

Risk management helps leaders see what's on the horizon, anticipate disruption and prepare for change. It has four core areas: **risk culture**, **risk committee**, **risk assessment** and **risk reporting**.

Risk culture

Risk culture is the foundation of effective risk management. It defines how people perceive, discuss and act on risk. A strong risk culture is about awareness, responsibility and sound judgement.

A healthy risk culture begins at the top. Leaders set the example through transparency, discipline and consistent decision-making. They demonstrate that managing risk is not a tick-box exercise but an integral part of running the business.

Key elements of a strong risk culture include:

- **Leadership commitment.** Executives and managers openly discuss risk, reward and accountability. Before committing to action, they ask: What could go wrong? What could go right?
- **Accountability.** Every employee understands their role in managing risk. Risk ownership sits with those closest to the activity, not just with the risk management function.
- **Open communication.** Employees are encouraged to escalate concerns early, without fear of blame. Mistakes are analysed for lessons, without judgement.
- **Decision discipline.** Major decisions include formal consideration of risk and opportunity, ensuring that risk-taking is deliberate, not accidental.
- **Training and awareness.** Regular education embeds risk thinking into daily work, from strategic planning to project execution.

A weak risk culture manifests in surprises, denial or overconfidence. A strong one is characterised by vigilance, curiosity and integrity. The strongest companies don't just manage risk; they talk about it continuously.

Risk committee

The risk committee provides formal oversight of risk management across the company. It ensures that material risks are identified, assessed, mitigated and monitored in a structured and consistent way.

Chaired by a senior board member or independent director, the risk committee reports directly to the board. In smaller organisations, it may be combined with the audit committee. In larger or regulated entities, it stands as a separate committee with defined authority and clear reporting lines.

Key responsibilities include:

- **Oversight of the risk framework.** Reviewing and approving the company's risk management framework, risk appetite statement and risk policies.
- **Monitoring key risks.** Reviewing enterprise-level risk registers, key emerging risks and mitigation plans on a regular basis.
- **Challenge and assurance.** Providing independent challenge to management's assessment of risk and effectiveness of controls.
- **Integration with strategy.** Ensuring risk considerations are embedded into decision-making, strategic planning, investment decisions and business cases.

- **Escalation.** Ensuring high or emerging risks are escalated promptly to the board for discussion.

The risk committee includes a balance of perspectives: finance, operations, legal, compliance and commercial. The committee should meet at least quarterly with structured agendas and documented minutes.

The most effective risk committees go beyond compliance reporting. They explore what could change, where the blind spots lie and how prepared the company is for disruption. They provide a productive space where difficult questions are asked.

Risk assessment

Risk assessment is the systematic process of identifying, analysing and evaluating risks that could impact the company's objectives. It brings structure and prioritisation to uncertainty, turning subjective concern into measurable insight.

The process follows five steps:

1. **Identify risks.** Through workshops, interviews, data analysis and incident reviews. The four key types of risk are strategic, operational, financial and compliance.
2. **Assess likelihood and impact.** Estimate how likely each risk is to occur and the severity of

its consequences. This can be qualitative (high/medium/low) or quantitative (financial value, probability).

3. **Evaluate controls.** Review the strength and effectiveness of existing controls; policies, systems or behaviours that prevent or mitigate risk.

4. **Determine residual risk.** After controls are considered, assess the remaining risk exposure. This reveals whether risk is within the company's risk appetite, ie which risks and what level of risk is acceptable to the board and senior management.

5. **Define response and mitigation.** Decide whether to tolerate, treat, transfer or avoid the risk (terminate), and assign clear ownership to senior management. More advanced risk functions use quantification of risks to feed directly into key leadership and board decision-making, using advanced probability calculations to support the potential financial impact of identified risks.

The results of this process are captured in a risk register, a structured list of key risks, controls, actions and responsible owners. The register is a living document that evolves as new risks emerge and existing ones change in nature or likelihood.

Risk assessments should not be static or annual exercises; they must be dynamic and integrated into decision-making. For example, launching a new product, entering a new market or implementing a new system should all trigger a fresh risk assessment.

Basic risk functions start with risk registers and risk heat maps to list and visualise risk exposure across the business.[28] More advanced risk functions are increasingly deploying probability models (eg using Monte Carlo), data analytics and AI to identify patterns, anomalies and early warning signals. The quantification and integration of risk into decision-making is considered best practice.[29] The goal is foresight; seeing trouble before it arrives.

Risk reporting

Risk reporting provides visibility and assurance across a business. It ensures leaders at every level understand the company's current risk profile and make informed decisions accordingly. Good risk reporting turns complex data into clear insights.

Effective risk reporting includes:

- **Executive risk dashboards.** Concise summaries of top risks, status of mitigations and emerging trends.

- **Risk appetite monitoring.** Comparing current risk exposures to the company's defined appetite and tolerance levels, ensuring alignment with strategy.
- **Incident and loss reporting.** Tracking operational incidents, near misses and control failures to identify root causes and prevent recurrence.
- **Thematic analysis.** Highlighting systemic issues across departments, such as repeated control weaknesses.
- **Integrated decision-making.** Presenting risk data and quantification to support key decision-making by senior management and the board.
- **Escalation and communication.** Clear thresholds for when issues are reported to the risk committee or board, ensuring timely awareness and action.

Good reporting focuses attention on the most material risks while maintaining traceability to the underlying detail.

Risk reporting also supports transparency to external stakeholders, investors, regulators, auditors and partners. Mature companies integrate risk reporting with performance and strategy dashboards, creating a single view on risk.

Risk management is not about eliminating risk but learning to survive and thrive with it. It enables confident decision-making by balancing ambition with caution. Risk is a language of leadership, a shared understanding of how to protect, adapt and achieve success in a world that is constantly changing.

Ethics & compliance

Ethics & compliance (E&C) ensures that the business does the right thing, not just meets legal and regulatory requirements. E&C defines the standards of behaviour expected from employees, building trust and protecting reputation. Today integrity is scrutinised more than ever and transparency is highly valued. Ethical businesses must win trust and loyalty.

Ethics & compliance is divided into four interconnected areas: **regulatory compliance**, **code of conduct**, **compliance monitoring** and **compliance reporting**.

Regulatory compliance

Regulatory compliance ensures the company meets the legal and regulatory requirements of the jurisdictions in which it operates. It protects the company from financial penalties, reputational harm and the erosion of trust with stakeholders.

Every industry operates under a network of regulations: financial services under anti-money laundering and securities laws, manufacturing under product safety and environmental standards, healthcare under patient and data protection laws.

Effective regulatory compliance includes:

- **Compliance framework.** A structured system that identifies all applicable laws and regulations, assigns ownership and tracks compliance.
- **Compliance risk assessment.** Evaluating where breaches are most likely to occur and their potential impact. This helps prioritise monitoring and resources.
- **Policies and procedures.** Translating regulatory obligations into clear internal rules, ensuring employees know what is required and why.
- **Training and awareness.** Regular training tailored to roles and compliance risk exposure. Employees must understand both the law and the company's specific expectations.

- **Regulatory monitoring.** Laws and regulations change and evolve. A strong compliance function tracks changes, assesses impact and updates policies accordingly.

A mature compliance approach integrates with other functions such as risk management, legal, internal audit and human resources to ensure alignment and avoid duplication. The objective is to comply and to build and maintain a culture that values compliance as a collective responsibility.

Code of conduct

A code of conduct defines the moral and behavioural standards expected of everyone in the company and often those connected to it, eg partners or suppliers. It is the ethical compass that guides decision-making and enforces the company's values.

A good code of conduct is clear, accessible and practical. It goes beyond policies and regulations, explaining how employees are expected to act in everyday situations.

Topics include:

- **Integrity and fair dealing.** Acting honestly and avoiding misleading practices.

- **Conflicts of interest.** Disclosing and managing situations where personal interests may influence professional judgement.
- **Anti-bribery and corruption.** Prohibiting all forms of bribery, facilitation payments or improper influence.
- **Confidentiality and data protection.** Respecting privacy, and safeguarding company, employee and customer information.
- **Equal opportunity and respect.** Promoting diversity, inclusion and respectful workplace behaviour.
- **Use of company assets.** Ensuring resources are used responsibly and only for legitimate business purposes.
- **Reporting misconduct.** Providing channels for employees to raise concerns safely, often through a whistleblowing hotline.

A code of conduct must be supported by leadership. When leaders demonstrate ethical behaviour, for example declining questionable deals, addressing misconduct openly or prioritising fairness over short-term gain, the right tone is set.

A code of conduct is a contract. It reinforces the idea that the company's reputation is built on the actions of every individual, every day.

Compliance monitoring

Compliance monitoring ensures that policies, procedures and compliance controls are functioning as intended. It provides ongoing assurance that the company's commitments to compliance are being met in practice, not just on paper.

Monitoring activities include:

- **Control testing.** Periodic reviews of high-risk processes (eg payments, procurement, data protection) to confirm compliance with policies and regulatory standards.
- **Thematic reviews.** Reviews into specific compliance areas, such as anti-money laundering, trade sanctions or insider dealing.
- **Surveillance and data analytics.** Automated systems that detect anomalies or potential breaches, such as unusual transactions or conflicts of interest.
- **Third-party oversight.** Assessing suppliers, agents and partners for compliance with ethical and legal standards.
- **Follow-up and remediation.** Tracking issues identified during monitoring, and ensuring corrective actions are implemented promptly.

Compliance monitoring should be risk-based, focused where the compliance exposure is greatest, and collaborative, not punitive. The goal is to identify weaknesses early, support improvement and maintain confidence that controls are effective.

A strong compliance function works closely with the business, providing practical guidance and easy escalation routes. It promotes partnership, not policing, helping teams meet objectives while staying within regulatory and ethical boundaries.

Compliance reporting

Compliance reporting brings transparency to senior management, the board and regulators. It demonstrates how well the company is managing its compliance risks and where improvements are needed.

Key elements include:

- **Regular management reports.** Summarising compliance status, breaches, training completion and open actions. Reports should highlight both progress and concern areas.
- **Incident and breach logs.** Recording all confirmed or suspected breaches, their root causes and remediation steps.
- **Regulatory reporting.** Submitting required filings, disclosures and self-assessments

accurately and on time. Regulators expect timely notification of material incidents.

- **Escalation framework.** Ensuring serious issues, such as fraud, corruption or systemic control failure, are promptly escalated to the board or relevant subcommittee.
- **Board and audit committee dashboards.** Visualising trends in compliance performance, training coverage and issue closure rates to facilitate informed oversight.

Effective compliance reporting converts monitoring data into insight and drives accountability across functions. The emphasis is on clarity and relevance, providing decision-makers with the information they need to act.

Transparency builds trust. Regulators value openness, employees respect honesty and shareholders gain confidence that integrity is being safeguarded.

Environment, social, governance

Environment, social, governance (ESG) elevates a company beyond transactions and profit, focusing on its impact on people and the planet. Investors, customers and employees increasingly expect businesses to act responsibly, and ESG frameworks measure and prove that commitment. By embedding sustainability, social responsibility and ethical leadership, companies strengthen their mandate and secure their place in the future economy.

ESG has four key areas: **sustainability & environmental impact**, **ESG data analytics**, **stakeholder engagement** and **ESG reporting**.

Sustainability & environmental impact

Sustainability & environmental impact addresses how the business uses resources, manages waste and contributes to the health of the planet. It balances growth with stewardship, ensuring that today's success does not come at tomorrow's expense.

The foundation is a clear sustainability policy, endorsed by leadership and integrated with corporate strategy. This policy sets out commitments on carbon reduction, resource efficiency and environmental protection.

Key areas include:

- **Carbon emissions.** Measuring and reducing greenhouse gas emissions where commercially possible. This includes direct emissions from operations, energy used and emissions from the supply chain.

- **Energy and resource efficiency.** Implementing energy-saving initiatives, water conservation and waste-reduction programmes. Efficiency reduces both environmental impact and operating cost, with a beneficial commercial outcome.
- **Circular economy practices.** Redesigning products and processes to recycle and reuse materials, minimise waste and extend product life cycles.
- **Sustainable procurement.** Working with suppliers who meet ethical and environmental standards, integrating sustainability criteria into sourcing decisions.
- **Biodiversity and land use.** Assessing and mitigating impacts on local ecosystems, especially in 'heavy' industries such as construction, manufacturing and energy.

Sustainability must be measurable. Targets should be specific, time-bound and linked to corporate objectives, such as achieving net zero by a defined year or reducing energy use per unit of output. Progress should be tracked, verified and communicated consistently. All of this is a significant challenge – this is where ESG data analytics comes in.

ESG data analytics

ESG data analytics provides evidence to support ESG commitments. Without accurate and reliable data, sustainability goals remain statements of intent rather than demonstrable performance.

ESG data collection covers a wide range of metrics across the environmental, social and governance spectrum. Examples include:

- **Environmental.** Carbon emissions, energy use, waste generation, recyclable content and water consumption.
- **Social.** Employee turnover, diversity ratios, training hours, community investment and health & safety incidents.
- **Governance.** Board diversity, executive pay alignment, ethics violations and policy compliance rates.

Data must be accurate, consistent and comparable. Companies need clear definitions, reporting boundaries (eg how far down the supply chain is monitored), and controlled data-collection processes. Increasingly, companies use digital platforms to centralise ESG data, automate collection from business systems and apply analytics to identify trends or outliers.

Analytics enable insights, highlighting areas of risk, inefficiency or opportunity. For example, analysing supplier carbon footprints may reveal concentration risks in the value chain, while workforce data may expose underrepresented demographics that limit innovation.

In mature businesses, ESG analytics are integrated into executive dashboards, linking sustainability performance directly to financial and operational results. This integration transforms ESG from a reporting obligation into a management tool for strategic decision-making.

Stakeholder engagement

Stakeholder engagement ensures a company's ESG priorities reflect the stakeholders it affects. These stakeholders include not just investors but employees, customers, suppliers, regulators and the communities the business operates in. Each group sees the company differently and has its own expectations.

The process starts with a materiality assessment. This is a structured way of figuring out which ESG issues matter to the company and its stakeholders, rather than guessing or following trends. A bank might focus heavily on data privacy and responsible lending, while a manufacturing company will prioritise emissions, energy use and ethical sourcing in its supply chain.

Effective stakeholder engagement follows these common principles:

- **Transparency.** Being open about goals, progress and where the company is struggling. Stakeholders can sense when something is wrong.
- **Inclusiveness.** Bringing in a range of voices, especially the people who feel the impact of operations most directly.
- **Responsiveness.** Listening and acting on feedback and showing how it shaped decisions builds credibility with stakeholders.
- **Consistency.** Ensuring that what the company says publicly matches what is happening internally. Misalignment quickly loses trust.
- **Partnership.** Working with regulators and industry peers where it makes sense, especially on challenges that are too big for any single company to tackle alone.

When done well, stakeholder engagement builds trust and turns stakeholders into supporters. People will back a company when they can see their concerns are heard and genuinely influence decisions.

ESG reporting

ESG reporting demonstrates how a company takes responsibility for the impact it has on the world. It shows where ESG sits in the business, how it is governed and what is happening day to day.

Most companies follow recognised reporting frameworks so what they disclose can be compared and trusted. The main ones include:

- **Global Reporting Initiative.**[30] A broad set of disclosures covering ESG topics.
- **Sustainability Accounting Standards Board.**[31] Industry-specific metrics that focus on what investors care about.
- **Task Force on Climate-related Financial Disclosures.**[32] Guidance on climate governance, climate risks and scenario planning.
- **Corporate Sustainability Reporting Directive**[33] **and European Sustainability Reporting Standards.**[34] The new generation of mandatory standards that are pushing ESG reporting into the mainstream.

Effective ESG reporting includes these important elements:

- Clear ownership of ESG at the leadership and governance level.

- Consistently measured data, with year-on-year trends rather than one-off numbers.
- Independent assurance over ESG metrics, not just a glossy narrative.
- A realistic view of progress, including targets missed and achieved.
- A candid explanation of the challenges the company faces, because not everything is perfect and pretending otherwise reduces credibility.

Transparent ESG reporting builds trust with stakeholders. Investors want to know the business isn't hiding anything, regulators want clarity and the public expects honesty. Increasingly, companies are putting their ESG disclosures inside their annual reports rather than in separate sustainability booklets, showing how mainstream this has become. Sustainability isn't a 'nice to have' anymore; it is an indicator of resilience, long-term thinking and quality of management.

ESG reporting verifies whether the company is acting responsibly and balancing value creation with its ethical, social and environmental obligations. It reflects how the company operates and what it stands for.

Internal audit

Internal audit provides independent assurance that things are working as they should. It tests controls, highlights development areas and drives improvements across the business. Internal audit gives the board and shareholders the confidence that the company is compliant, effective, efficient and secure. It is a trusted adviser supporting sustainable success.

Internal audit helps the business learn, adapt and strengthen through evidence-based assurance. The function has four key areas: **independence & objectivity**, **audit committee**, **aligned assurance** and **audit engagements**.

Independence & objectivity

Independence & objectivity are the cornerstones of internal audit. Without them, the assurance that internal audit provides loses credibility. What do we mean by these terms?

Organisational independence means that internal audit operates outside of management's direct control. The chief audit executive (CAE) reports functionally to the audit committee of the board, and administratively to the CEO. This reporting line ensures that audit findings are not suppressed or influenced by those being audited.

Objectivity requires auditors to perform their work free from bias, conflict of interest or undue influence. Internal auditors must maintain professional scepticism, questioning evidence, validating data and avoiding assumptions.

To safeguard independence & objectivity:

- The internal audit charter must clearly define internal audit's purpose, authority and responsibilities. It should be approved by the audit committee and reviewed annually.
- The function should have unrestricted access to all information, systems and employees relevant to its work.
- Auditors must not design or operate controls they later review, as doing so would compromise independence.

- The CAE must have the authority to escalate concerns directly to the audit committee or board chair if independence is threatened.

Professional standards, such as The Institute of Internal Auditors' (IIA) International Professional Practices Framework (IPPF),[35] provide globally recognised principles and guidance for maintaining integrity, competence and objectivity in all audit work.

Independence does not mean isolation. Internal audit must remain close enough to the business to understand its risks and operations but distant enough to evaluate them impartially. It is a careful balancing act.

Audit committee

The audit committee provides oversight and direction for the internal audit function. It ensures that assurance work is objective, risk-based and aligned with the board's priorities.

Core responsibilities include:

- **Approving the internal audit charter and plan.** Reviewing the scope, coverage and resources of internal audit to ensure the correct focus on key risks.

- **Reviewing reports and findings.** Evaluating internal audit results, management responses and the timely completion of corrective actions.
- **Monitoring independence.** Ensuring the CAE has sufficient authority, budget and access to perform duties without interference.
- **Coordinating assurance.** Overseeing interactions between internal and external auditors and other assurance providers to ensure efficiency and avoid duplication.
- **Performance evaluation.** Annually assessing the effectiveness of internal audit, supported by external quality assessments at least every five years, in line with IIA standards.

The relationship between the CAE and the audit committee chair is key. Regular confidential meetings enable open discussion of emerging risks, sensitive findings and organisational culture.

An effective audit committee focuses on what has gone wrong and whether the company is learning from what has been found. It promotes accountability, transparency and a continuous improvement culture.

Internal audit is the company's independent conscience. It provides assurance that controls are working, risks are managed and governance is effective. It also helps the business evolve, identifying opportunities for efficiency, effectiveness and resilience.

Aligned assurance

Aligned assurance ensures that the various assurance functions within the company – risk management, compliance, quality, health & safety, information security and internal audit – work in a coordinated effort, avoiding any duplication.

Without alignment, assurance can become fragmented: multiple reviews of the same process, inconsistent findings or unaddressed gaps. Aligned assurance brings coherence, efficiency and clarity.

Key principles include:

- **Three lines of defence.**[36] Management owns and manages risk (first line of defence), risk and compliance provide oversight (second line), and internal audit provides independent assurance (third line). Each line is distinct but interconnected.
- **Assurance mapping.** A structured approach to understand who provides assurance over which risks, processes or controls. It identifies overlaps and blind spots, allowing the audit committee to direct appropriately.
- **Shared planning.** Regular coordination meetings between assurance functions to align plans, share findings and agree on priorities.

- **Coordinated reporting.** Developing a unified assurance view for the board and audit committee, combining insights from all assurance functions to give a holistic picture of governance and control effectiveness.

Aligned assurance reduces fatigue within the business by eliminating duplicate requests and ensures senior leaders receive a single, coherent view of the health of the company.

When assurance functions are aligned, the board gains confidence that risks are being managed comprehensively and that assurance resources are used effectively.

Audit engagements

Internal audit broadly performs two types of engagements: assurance and advisory. Both add value and improve operations but they differ in focus and approach.

Assurance engagements evaluate the adequacy and effectiveness of governance, risk management and control processes. These audits are risk-based, determined by a risk assessment of the business and an annual audit plan approved by the audit committee. The audit plan focuses on areas of highest risk to the business.

Assurance engagements follow five stages:

1. **Planning.** Defining objectives, scope, timeframe, assessment criteria and risk focus areas.
2. **Fieldwork.** Testing controls, interviewing stakeholders, reviewing data and validating evidence provided by management.
3. **Reporting.** Communicating findings, conclusions and recommendations with clarity and risk prioritisation.
4. **Wrap-up.** Closing the audit file, ensuring audit evidence and supporting documentation is secured, and conducting performance evaluations and stakeholder feedback surveys.
5. **Follow-up.** Verifying that agreed actions are implemented and effective by the dates committed to by management during the audit.

Advisory engagements provide guidance to improve governance or processes before risks materialise. They are collaborative and forward-looking. Examples include pre-implementation reviews of new systems; policy, procedure or process redesign; and benchmarking processes to best practice.

Advisory work must be conducted carefully to preserve independence. Internal audit advises management on good practice but should not assume responsibility for operational decisions.

Across both assurance and advisory work, internal audit's value lies in its balanced perspective, identifying weaknesses while recognising strengths and helping the company learn from both.

QUESTIONS FOR YOU

1. How confident are you that your company sees risk clearly? Not just the risks on paper, but the risks people hesitate to talk about.
2. When pressure rises, how consistently does your company choose the ethical path, or where do values bend to convenience, speed or commercial targets?
3. Do your assurance functions – risk, compliance, ESG and internal audit – operate in alignment or do they work in silos that create blind spots, duplication or confusion?

Take some time to reflect on what you have learned so far.

Key learnings

1. **Assurance brings discipline, clarity and accountability**
   Risk, E&C, ESG and internal audit ensure decisions stand up to scrutiny, values are upheld under pressure and the company remains resilient as it grows.
2. **A strong risk culture is more important than any framework or heat map**
   The power of risk management lies in open communication, curiosity and psychological safety. When people escalate issues early and speak honestly about uncertainty, leaders make better decisions.
3. **Ethical behaviour must be lived, not written**
   Codes of conduct, policies and training mean little unless leaders demonstrate integrity. Ethics is a daily choice, and compliance relies on clarity, transparency and trust.
4. **ESG is now a strategic lens, not only a reporting obligation**
   Environmental impact, social responsibility and governance structures influence investor confidence, partnerships and long-term value creation. ESG must be measurable, embedded and supported by reliable data.
5. **Assurance functions must align to give the board a single, coherent view of risk.**
   When risk, compliance, ESG and internal audit operate in silos, blind spots grow. Aligned assurance avoids duplication, reduces assurance fatigue in the business and provides leadership with a unified picture of how well the company is being run.

Final thoughts

For more details and free content on the Assure stage, please visit Standardmodelforbusiness.com. Scan the QR code:

With assurance established and trust secured, we now turn our attention to how businesses are financed at each stage of their journey, from the first spark of an idea to becoming a listed, mature enterprise.

CHAPTER SEVEN

Financing

CHAPTER SEVEN

Financing

I was auditing the business planning function of a large semiconductor manufacturer at the company's headquarters in San Francisco, the most important assurance reviews in the business. The company was preparing for an ambitious multi-year expansion plan: new technology, new fabrication capability, new markets. Capital expenditure ran into the billions, requiring a complex mix of shareholder funding and debt. Everything depended on the forecasts.

The planning team had built a five-year financial model. It looked optimistic. Volumes climbed sharply, yields improved as hoped, demand rose quarterly. By year three, the company would be unstoppable. The tone of this financial model was unmistakable: everything goes right.

On the second day of the audit, we reviewed the revenue assumptions and noticed the ramp-up was too steep. The customer pipeline was too perfect, the yields assumed immediate efficiency and the timing of the revenue aligned too neatly with when the business needed the money.

The model wasn't built around reality, it was built around hope.

I paused the meeting. 'Let's assume revenue is 10% lower than forecast. What happens?'

No one spoke.

The percentage is small, but for this company 10% was $500 million. It's a deviation that happens frequently: a product delay, a customer pushing orders into the next quarter, a supply constraint, a shift in demand, a competitor moving faster.

The downside was not fully considered: no alternative case, no sensitivity analysis. The entire financing plan – the debt, the repayments, the shareholder injections – was built on a single, optimistic future.

Over the next few days, the team explored alternative cases. What if yields improved more slowly? What if demand softened? What if one major customer delayed orders?

The base case still looked strong in each case, but the vulnerabilities and risks became visible. The company adjusted its plans to become more resilient and honest. It was an important lesson in finance learned that year.

Financing a company, whether a start-up or a global semiconductor giant, requires a disciplined understanding of uncertainty. Cash, debt, shareholders, capital markets all depend on the same thing: a truthful forecast.

The company planned on listing on a stock exchange as an initial public offering (IPO), making it vital to address the business planning, forecasting and financial planning early.

All companies, regardless of size, need to know the numbers and stress test their projections. Potential investors and finance providers will do exactly that too.

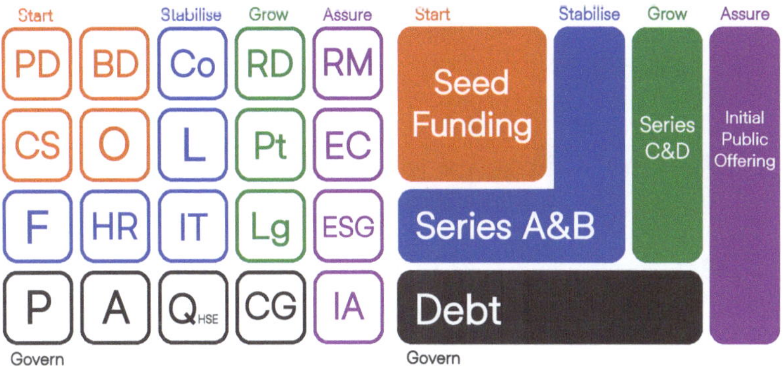

Financing matches a company's ambitions with the capital required to achieve them. It is the process of securing funds to progress the business. Investors take some ownership of the business in exchange for risking their capital. At each stage, investors, lenders and markets ask: Do we believe in this idea? Can the business operate with discipline? Can it scale? Can it control risk?

The Standard Model for Business provides a clear map for that journey. As a company moves from Start to Stabilise, Grow, Govern and finally Assure, its financing needs and options evolve. Early on, capital is scarce and belief driven. Later, it becomes more abundant but also more demanding, with strict investor expectations for governance, transparency and performance. These financing options map to each stage of The Standard Model for Business as an overlay (see figure above).

In this chapter, we will follow that progression:

1. **Start: Seed funding.**[37] Turning ideas into prototypes and early progress.
2. **Stabilise: Series A&B.**[38] Building the backbone of the business, the teams and systems that create more stability and repeatable performance.
3. **Grow: Series C&D.**[39] Scaling into new markets, products and geographies, while protecting the company's economics and culture.

4. **Govern: Debt financing.**[40] Using leverage and capital structure as tools of control, not speculation.

5. **Assure: IPO.**[41] Preparing to enter public markets, where the company's numbers, narrative and governance are tested under full scrutiny.

For each stage of financing, I will present three key areas: **purpose**, **good practices** and **risks & realities**.

Common good practices include:

- **Clear economics.** The company understands its margins, customer acquisition costs, retention rates and customer lifetime value. Decisions are based more on data rather than instinct.
- **Consistent cash flow and profitability.** The company has stable cash flow and profitability year on year. It can forecast revenue, costs and working capital reliably, giving investors and lenders confidence in its ability to meet obligations.
- **Financial discipline.** Budgeting, procurement, treasury and operations are aligned. The business treats investment and leverage responsibly.

Common risks & realities for all stages of financing include:

- **Poor finances.** Inaccurate reporting, weak forecasting, late management accounts or no cash discipline. These undermine investor confidence.
- **Misalignment with investors.** Overpromising and under-delivering, hiding challenges or shifting strategy without alignment. This erodes trust and complicates future fundraising.
- **Overconfidence in cash flow.** Having too optimistic cash forecasts. Unexpected downturns, cost spikes or delayed customer payments can test the company's ability to repay.
- **Cultural misalignment.** Employees accustomed to start-up freedom may struggle with the governance and documentation required of a public company.

Companies that attract capital on the best terms are those that understand uncertainty, stress test their plans and align financing decisions with strategy, risk and governance. Financing is about building a resilient relationship between ambition, cash flow and control that allows the business to endure.

Start: Seed funding

Seed funding brings a start-up idea into the real world. At this stage, capital is scarce, uncertainty is high and the company is little more than an idea. That is why seed funding matters: it gives founders the resources to test whether the idea deserves to survive and thrive.

Purpose

The purpose of seed funding is to prove feasibility of an idea. It is about gathering early evidence that the idea works, customers care about what you are selling, the economics make sense and the product can be delivered repeatably.

At this stage, investors back possibility not certainty. They invest in the founders, the market insight and the clarity of thinking. Seed funding exists to answer several big questions:

- Is the problem real and urgent?
- Does the proposed solution resonate with real customers?
- Can the team deliver what they promise?
- Is there a business model that might scale later?

Seed funding creates the first bridge between concept and traction. It gives founders enough runway to learn quickly, refine their idea and build credibility for the next round of funding.

Good practices

Good seed-stage companies focus relentlessly on learning, clarity and discipline. They avoid the temptation to build too much, hire too fast or market too widely. Seed funding typically involves a handful of essential building blocks that move the business from idea to reality.

This stage should include:

- **Sharp focus on the core problem.** Founders understand the problem better than anyone else. They talk to customers constantly, refine assumptions and adjust based on real evidence.
- **MVP.** A simple, functional version of the product or service that allows the team to observe real customer behaviour. Not perfect; just enough to test the idea.
- **Early customer validation.** Conversations, pilots, prototypes, sign-ups or early sales that indicate genuine demand.
- **A small, capable, committed team.** The team is lean but effective, with complementary skills. Everyone is close to the work. At this stage, seed investors invest more in the team than the product or service.
- **Frugality and cash discipline.** Seed capital is treated like oxygen. Budgets are simple, spending is thoughtful and the burn rate is controlled. The company buys time to learn and adjust.

Seed-stage companies that master these components create credibility. They establish the foundations needed to raise institutional capital in the next round of funding, series A.

Risks & realities

Seed funding is the riskiest stage of a company's life. Most early-stage businesses do not reach sufficient scale because execution, timing or discipline falter.

Common risks include:

- **Building without testing.** Founders fall in love with features or technology and avoid uncomfortable truths from customers.
- **Overestimating demand.** Positive conversations with customers are mistaken for willingness to buy. Many seed-stage products fail because the market does not care enough.
- **Weak or divided founding team.** Misalignment between founders erodes focus, speed and trust. It is one of the most common reasons startups fail.[42]
- **Ignoring the business model.** Even at the seed stage, founders must address how the company might make money. Hoping for scale without economics is not a business plan.

Seed-stage companies succeed when founders embrace reality early on. They learn quickly, adapt boldly and protect their scarce resources. Seed funding does not prove that the company will work; it proves that it *might*, and that the team is worth backing.

Stabilise: Series A&B

Series A&B mark the transition from a promising idea to a functioning business. These funding rounds are about evidence, structure and repeatability. Investors now expect discipline. They want to see that the product works, customers are returning and operations can scale without chaos.

This is where the company shifts from founder-driven improvisation to professionalised execution. It builds the systems, teams and controls that allow growth to happen consistently and safely.

Purpose

The purpose of series A is to build capability. It takes a small, energetic start-up and turns it into a company with structure, expertise and the foundations of a disciplined organisation. At series A, the question is no longer 'Does the idea work?' but 'Can the business work every day, reliably?'

Series B takes this one step further. Its purpose is to scale what is already working through repeatable processes. This funding accelerates go-to-market efforts, deepens operational capacity and expands the company into new segments or geographies.

Together, series A&B answer the critical question: Can this company grow without losing control?

These rounds build the backbone of the business; systems, leadership, unit economics and culture, so that later-stage capital can be used for expanding upon a solid foundation.

Good practices

A strong series-A&B-stage company demonstrates maturity, discipline and consistency. It evolves from a founder-led project to a professionally run business without losing the creative spark that made it successful. Series A&B involve several building blocks that move the company from a promising start-up to a stable operator.

Good practices include:

- **Consistent, repeatable operations.** Processes are stabilised. The delivery of the product or service becomes predictable. Customer experience is reliable and repeatable.
- **Strengthened leadership team.** Founders hire specialists: a CFO, CTO, head of sales or other key roles. Leadership becomes deeper, more capable and more rounded.
- **Scalable systems and infrastructure.** IT systems, HR processes, financial reporting and compliance structures mature. The business upgrades from spreadsheets to systems.
- **Disciplined performance management.** KPIs, dashboards and weekly meetings replace improvised decision-making. Leadership can see more clearly what is happening across the business.
- **Professional investor communications.** Board meetings are structured. Reporting is accurate. Results are transparent. Investor confidence builds.
- **Strengthened financial management.** Forecasting improves. Cash flow is monitored closely. Management accounts are timely and accurate. The company begins behaving like an institution rather than a project.

- **Brand, marketing and growth engine.** Marketing matures into a structured function with clearer channels, performance metrics and predictable acquisition strategies.
- **Culture and organisational development.** As headcount grows, culture becomes intentional rather than accidental. Values are articulated, leadership sets tone and internal communication improves.

At series A&B, investors look for a company that behaves like it is ready to scale operationally, financially and culturally. These good practices form the foundation for later growth. Without them, the next rounds of funding (series C&D) can be wasted.

Risks & realities

Series A&B come with their own challenges. Common risks include:

- **Growing too fast, too soon.** Hiring ahead of revenue, expanding into new markets without readiness or scaling sales without strong unit economics.
- **Losing focus.** Chasing too many opportunities at once. Trying to do too much too soon, which reduces the value proposition.

- **Incomplete or weak systems.** Using makeshift tools and spreadsheets for too long. Failing to invest in the required infrastructure. This creates operational problems that become expensive to fix.
- **Cultural friction.** Rapid hiring introduces new personalities, expectations and working styles. Without clear leadership, culture can become fragmented.

Series A&B are where discipline takes hold. Companies that invest early in structure, capability and clarity are the ones that rise into the Grow stage without losing their footing.

Grow: Series C&D

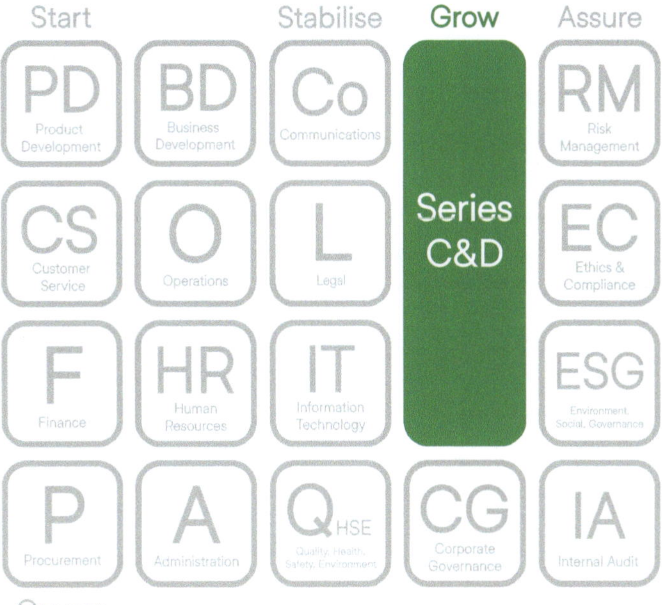

Series C&D mark the acceleration phase of a company's journey. By this point, the business is no longer proving itself, it has evidence, customers, systems and a leadership team capable of strong execution. These funding rounds are about scaling confidently, strengthening the company, entering new markets and preparing for major strategic events such as acquisitions or an eventual IPO.

Series A&B test repeatability and series C&D test momentum. The question now becomes: Can this company grow at scale, across borders and under scrutiny without losing quality, economics or control?

Purpose

The purpose of series C is to expand aggressively and capitalise on proven success. The business model works, the economics are strong and the market opportunity is meaningful. Series C gives the business the resources to capture that opportunity ahead of competitors.

The purpose of series D is more strategic. It strengthens the balance sheet, deepens international presence, supports acquisitions or prepares the company for IPO readiness. Series D often acts as a bridge between private growth and the public markets.

Together, these rounds answer the question: Can this company become a global leader, not just a successful business?

These rounds take the company from strong to dominant, from national to international and from 'growing fast' to 'operating at scale'.

Good practices

A strong series-C&D-stage company demonstrates operational maturity, global potential and institutional-level discipline. It must perform even while growing quickly. Series C&D investors require the company to build upon its foundation with deeper, more scalable structures and processes.

What good looks like at this stage:

- **International-ready operations.** The company can operate reliably across borders, cultures and regulatory environments. Processes are standardised but adaptable.
- **Strengthened governance and reporting.** Boards formalise, committees strengthen, financial reporting is fast and accurate, and internal controls resemble those of a global, mature company.
- **Powerful growth engine.** Sales and marketing are highly structured, data-driven and capable of delivering predictable pipeline at scale.
- **Advanced technology and infrastructure.** Systems are robust, automated and integrated.

Data flows cleanly across the organisation. Technology becomes a growth enabler, not a bottleneck.

- **Leadership with global capability.** Executives are hired with experience in scaling companies, entering new markets and managing large teams. Leadership now resembles that of a mature multinational.
- **Clear strategic narrative.** The company knows who it is, where it is going and how it will win, with a clear and articulated strategy. This narrative aligns all stakeholders.
- **Product and portfolio expansion**. Investment goes into new product lines, adjacent services or R&D initiatives that expand the total addressable market. Innovation becomes structured rather than experimental.
- **Brand and market leadership.** Marketing shifts focus from customer acquisition to brand building: reputation, credibility and trust. The company works to become a recognised leader in its category.
- **Mergers & acquisitions.** C-stage companies begin acquiring complementary businesses, technology assets or regional players. D-stage companies often explore vertical integration (buying suppliers and/or distributors).

Companies at this stage behave like professional institutions. They operate with discipline, analyse performance in real time and manage risk intentionally. Series C&D prepare the business for the demands of institutional capital markets, not just in performance but in professionalism.

Risks & realities

This is the stage where successful companies can stumble, because scale introduces complexity.

Common risks include:

- **Losing operational control.** Processes break under the weight of growth. Quality drops. Customer experience suffers. Execution becomes inconsistent.
- **International missteps.** Cultural misalignment, regulatory failures, weak local leadership and poor localisation strategies can slow or stop global expansion.
- **Strategic drift.** Ambition leads to overreach: too many products, too many markets, too many initiatives. The company loses its strategic focus.
- **Leadership gaps.** The skills needed to reach $5 million in revenue are not the skills needed to reach $500 million. Companies that delay upgrading leadership often stall.

- **Integration failures.** Acquisitions can weaken the business if integration is slow, culturally incompatible or poorly executed.

Series C&D investors demand maturity. They require a company to think like a global leader, with the governance, discipline and systems to match. Those who master this stage enter the Govern stage with confidence and legitimacy.

Govern: Debt

Debt financing marks the stage where a company begins using leverage strategically. By this point, the organisation has evidence of stability: predictable revenue, functioning operations and governance strong enough to satisfy external scrutiny. Debt becomes a financial instrument of efficiency, discipline and control.

Unlike equity, debt does not dilute ownership. It is a flexible way of financing a company's growth but it also demands maturity. Debt is a great tool for the disciplined and a dangerous one for those that are not.

Purpose

The purpose of debt financing is to enable growth without giving up further ownership. At this stage, investors, lenders and rating agencies expect the company to behave like a well-governed institution. Debt allows the company to amplify returns, smooth cash flow and finance major projects while maintaining control.

Debt answers a set of questions that are very different to equity funding rounds:

- Can the business generate consistent cash flows?
- Are governance and controls strong enough to give lenders confidence?

- Does the company use leverage wisely, without overextending?

Debt becomes part of the company's capital strategy. It optimises the cost of capital, funds expansion and signals maturity to stakeholders. A company ready for meaningful debt is a company ready to operate under tighter expectations.

Good practices

A strong Govern-stage company approaches debt with clarity, discipline and foresight. Lenders expect predictability, transparency and professionalism. Good companies deliver exactly that. Debt financing introduces concepts and instruments that differ from equity funding rounds.

Good practice at this stage includes:

- **Robust financial systems and controls.** The monthly financial close is timely. Forecasting is accurate. Internal controls are documented and effective. Management accounts are accurate and trusted.
- **Strong governance and transparency.** Boards are active, audit and risk committees operate effectively and reporting is consistent, accurate and well structured. Lenders value clarity.

- **Clear capital structure strategy.** Debt is intentionally sized and timed. Leadership understands the company's optimal mix of debt and equity, covenant thresholds and refinancing cycles.
- **Strong bank and lender relationships.** Communication is proactive. Issues are surfaced early. Trust between the company and banks is built through transparency and dialogue.
- **Covenants.** Debt agreements include covenants that set boundaries around financial health, including leverage ratios, interest coverage and minimum liquidity levels.
- **Creditworthiness and ratings.** For larger companies, credit ratings (eg from S&P or Moody's) influence borrowing cost. It is in the company's interest to have a strong credit rating (lower borrowing cost).

Companies that excel in this stage behave like public companies long before they become them. Debt becomes part of the operating rhythm of the business.

Risks & realities

Debt introduces leverage and leverage introduces pressure, as unlike equity, debt must be paid back on schedule. Used wisely, debt is a great financial tool.

Used poorly, it can destabilise even the strongest companies.

Common risks at this stage include:

- **Over-leveraging.** Too much debt reduces flexibility and raises the risk of covenant breaches, forcing difficult conversations with lenders or, in extreme cases, restructuring.
- **Weak forecasting and reporting.** If financial data is inaccurate, late or poorly controlled, the company risks breaching covenants or losing lender trust.
- **Rising interest rates.** Variable-rate loans introduce exposure to interest rate movements. Without hedging or diversification, financing costs can climb rapidly.
- **Lender relationship breakdown.** Poor communication, late reporting or hiding problems erode trust. Once lost, it is difficult to regain.
- **Strategic rigidity.** Debt can constrain flexibility. Heavily leveraged companies may be forced to delay investment, limit hiring or defer strategic decisions.

Debt can be a powerful catalyst for growth but only for companies with the discipline to manage it. It is the financial expression of governance: clear controls, strong reporting and leadership that treats obligations with seriousness and respect.

Companies that master debt financing build credibility with lenders and markets. They prepare themselves for the final stage of the financing journey: stepping into the public markets.

Assure: Initial public offering

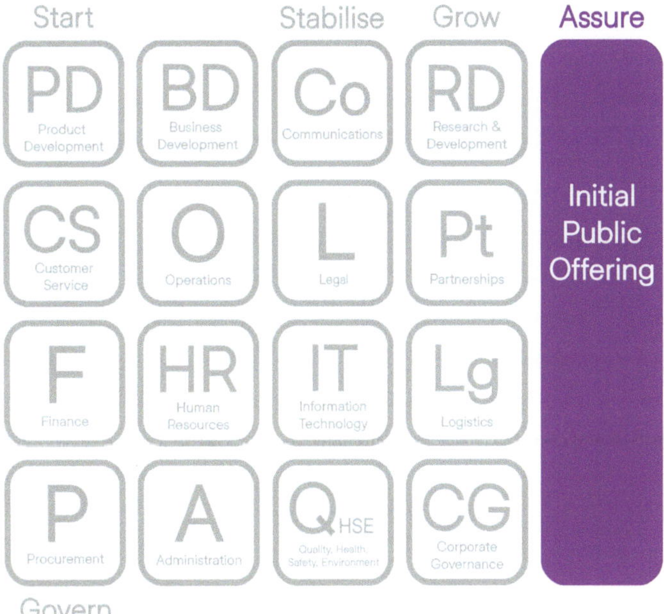

An IPO represents the culmination of a company's financing journey – the moment it steps from private enterprise into the public markets. It is both a milestone and a transformation. Listing on a stock exchange requires a level of transparency, discipline and maturity that exceeds anything demanded by investors in earlier stages.

An IPO is a way to raise capital. It is also a test of governance, culture, reporting and leadership. Public markets reward clarity and punish confusion. The markets value consistency over ambition, truth over optimism (most of the time) and discipline over improvisation.

Purpose

The purpose of an IPO is to raise capital at scale and to convert the company into a public institution capable of operating under scrutiny. It allows a business to fund major expansion, access new investor bases and provide liquidity for early shareholders. Importantly, an IPO forces the company to meet the expectations of public investors, accurate reporting, strong governance and a stable strategy.

An IPO answers a different set of questions than private financing:

- Can this company sustain performance quarter after quarter?
- Are governance structures strong enough for public oversight?

- Is financial reporting accurate, timely and trusted?
- Can leadership communicate transparently with the market?

The IPO becomes a public declaration that the company is ready to operate at institutional scale. It becomes a promise to shareholders, regulators, employees and the wider economy.

Good practices

Companies ready for an IPO demonstrate the highest maturity across operations, governance, financial reporting and culture. They behave like public companies long before leadership ring the bell on listing day. An IPO requires a significant coordinated effort across leadership, finance, legal, operations and external advisers. The process is demanding, multi-layered and time sensitive.

What good looks like at the IPO stage:

- **Consistent financial performance.** Revenue, margins, costs and cash flow are stable, predictable and supported by strong systems. Forecasts are credible and based on actual performance.
- **Robust governance framework.** A capable board with independent directors, active committees

(audit, risk, remuneration), and clear governance charters and documents. Decisions are clear in minutes of meetings.

- **High-quality financial reporting.** The monthly financial close is disciplined. Audits are clean. Internal controls are strong. The company meets IFRS or relevant financial reporting standards without issue.
- **Clear strategic narrative.** Leadership communicates the company's mission, growth strategy and long-term value creation clearly and confidently. The story aligns with the numbers.
- **Mature risk, compliance and ESG functions.** Public investors demand clarity on risks, ethics, sustainability and governance.
- **Cultural readiness for scrutiny.** Employees understand confidentiality and the importance of consistent messaging. Transparency is embraced, not feared.
- **Adviser selection and underwriting.** Investment banks help structure, price and market the IPO. Legal counsel ensures compliance. Auditors validate financials and IPO readiness. Communications advisers support messaging during the investor roadshow.

An IPO-ready company looks, feels and operates like a listed entity before it becomes one.

Risks & realities

Going public amplifies both strengths and weaknesses of a company. The transition is demanding and not all companies thrive once listed.

Common risks include:

- **Quarterly pressure and short-termism.** Public markets reward consistent short-term results. Companies may feel pressured to prioritise short-term performance over long-term value creation.
- **Loss of privacy and increased scrutiny.** Every decision, misstep or comment can move the share price. Leadership must operate transparently and cautiously.
- **Operational strain.** Reporting volume increases significantly. Internal teams must meet tight deadlines and be accurate.
- **Share price volatility.** External events, including interest rates, market sentiment or competitor actions, can affect valuation regardless of company performance.

An IPO is not the finish line, it is a new beginning under tighter scrutiny. Companies that succeed in the public markets are those that maintain discipline, communicate transparently and create long-term value.

QUESTIONS FOR YOU

1. If your revenue came in 10–20% lower than planned, what would happen to your business? Would you still be able to pay people, suppliers and lenders on time, or would something important start to break?
2. How is your business funded today? How does it match the stage your business is in? For example, are you still relying on friends and family when you really need more structured investors? Are you taking on bank debt before your cash flows are stable?
3. What would make a serious investor or lender hesitate about backing your business today?
4. Think about your numbers, systems, reporting and leadership culture. Where would potential investors see gaps or risk?
5. How much discipline do you have around cash today?
6. Do you have a simple, regular way of checking cash coming in and going out, or are you mostly relying on instinct and hope?

Take some time to reflect on what you have learned so far.

Key Learnings

1. **The most valuable forecast is the truthful one**
   Financing decisions that matter cannot be based on a single optimistic base case. Robust financing requires scenario thinking, downside testing and the humility to accept that the future will not unfold exactly as planned.

2. **Financing is a journey that must match the maturity of the business**
   From seed to series A/B, series C/D, debt and finally IPO, each stage asks a different question of the company: belief, stability, scale, control and assurance. Capital should be structured to fit where the business truly is on this path.
3. **The quality of financing is as important as the quantity**
   The right mix of equity, debt and internal cash flow has strategic importance. High valuations, large rounds and big facilities can be dangerous if they are not anchored in sound unit economics, disciplined spending and a clear path to sustainable cash generation.
4. **Financing relationships are tests of governance and credibility**
   Investors, lenders and eventually public markets do more than provide capital; they continuously assess how the business is run. Transparent reporting, honest communication and respect for covenants and obligations build trust, unlocking better terms, greater flexibility and long-term support.
5. **IPO-level discipline is useful even if you never list**
   Preparing for an IPO – be it audited numbers, strong controls, independent governance or clear narrative – is the highest expression of assurance. The same principles strengthen any company, whether it goes public or stays private. Financing done well is about building a business that can withstand scrutiny and endure.

Final thoughts

For more details and free content on financing, please visit Standardmodelforbusiness.com. Scan the QR code:

With financing understood and each stage of the journey complete, we now step back to see The Standard Model for Business as a whole and learn how these elements form a single, coherent model for business.

Conclusion: Bringing It All Together

The moment you reach this chapter, something important has happened. You have travelled through the entirety of The Standard Model for Business, from the spark of an idea in the **Start** stage, to the stabilising structures of **Stabilise**, to the engines of scale in **Grow**, through the discipline and safeguards of **Govern** and finally to the integrity and accountability of **Assure**. You have seen how companies progress, why they stall and what separates the promising from the exceptional.

This chapter ties the threads together. It distils the principles of this book, invites you to reflect on your career and challenges you to act. Knowledge alone does nothing; business is changed by those who put that knowledge to work.

Summary of key learnings

If you take only a handful of ideas from this book, let them be these:

- **Businesses grow through defined stages.** Every company – whether a start-up in a garage or a multinational with global operations – must progress through the five stages of The Standard Model for Business. The challenges evolve, the priorities shift and the skills required at each stage are different. Strength in one stage does not guarantee strength in another.
- **Execution beats enthusiasm.** You can have the best idea in the world, but without disciplined execution, systems, processes and governance, it will fail. The companies that win are those that combine creativity with discipline.
- **Culture is built through behaviour.** Every chapter of this book reinforces one truth: culture is shaped by what people actually do, not what a company claims. Quality, ethics, safety, risk, governance, customer service. These are all daily behaviours, not policies.
- **Assurance is not the end of the journey; it is what protects it.** Assurance functions, risk, compliance, ESG and internal audit do not slow companies down; they protect them, inform them and sharpen them. Assurance is the lens that keeps ambition honest and execution aligned.

- **Financing is the mirror that reflects maturity.** The way a company raises capital reveals how disciplined it is, how well it forecasts and how confident investors can be in its future. Financing is not a stage you reach, it is a responsibility you earn.

These ideas form the backbone of The Standard Model for Business. This conclusion is not just a recap; it is also about you.

Own your career

The most successful people in business are not those with the greatest credentials or the loudest opinions. They are the ones who take ownership of their development. They don't wait for opportunities; they prepare for them.

Owning your career means:

- Taking responsibility for your learning
- Seeking breadth, not just depth
- Understanding how the whole business works, not only your function
- Asking better questions, not just giving better answers
- Being the person who sees the bigger picture

In Chapter 1, I mentioned that a good generalist needs to grasp 80% of all areas of a business. This book is a good start, but your journey is far from over. Being a good generalist is difficult, perhaps more difficult than becoming a specialist in one area. However, it is worth it. The Standard Model for Business ecosystem is here to support you on your journey.

If you understand The Standard Model for Business, you already stand apart. You now see the common architecture beneath the surface of every business. You see how different functions interlock. You understand why companies succeed or fail.

This perspective is a competitive advantage. Use it.

Identify the gaps

Every ambitious professional has development gaps. The difference is that high performers identify them early and proactively work on them.

Ask yourself:

- Which of the five stages do I understand least?
- Which of the twenty functions have I never meaningfully interacted with?
- Which responsibilities of senior leaders still feel abstract to me?

- Where do I feel least confident speaking with experts?
- If I were promoted tomorrow, where would I be exposed?

Strong generalists rise faster because they can see across the organisation. Great leaders rise even faster because they can connect what they see.

Your gaps are not weaknesses; they are opportunities. They show you exactly where to learn next.

Training

Knowledge becomes power only when you put it into action. That is why I created free online resources to extend your learning beyond the pages of this book.

At the end of every chapter, you will find a QR code that links to my online platform at Standardmodelforbusiness.com. There you will find:

- Deeper insights into each of the twenty functions
- Expanded tools and frameworks
- Practical templates and checklists
- Case studies and examples
- Short videos explaining core concepts

- Free articles and guides
- Access to future courses, workshops and training programmes

This ecosystem is designed to grow with you. The book gives you the framework; the online material gives you the tools to apply it.

Whether you're preparing for your first management role, scaling a start-up or stepping into an executive position, the right training accelerates your progress. The best careers are built deliberately, not accidentally.

Next steps

Across these chapters, I have given you a single, coherent model for understanding business end-to-end. I have shown you:

- How companies evolve through the five stages
- How each function contributes to performance
- How systems and structures protect and enhance growth
- How governance and assurance maintain integrity
- How financing maps across every stage of the journey

I have shown you the business world as I have experienced it across 20+ years, multiple industries, continents, crises and transformations. More importantly, I have given you a way to make sense of that world: a map, a lens, a guide.

This book does not tell you what to think. It gives you the structure to think for yourself.

Knowledge without action is wasted potential, so here are your next steps:

1. **Pick one function you want to master next.** Start there. Learn its language. Understand its purpose. You do not need to become an expert, just competent enough to engage experts with confidence.
2. **Map your company to The Standard Model.** Identify which stage it is in today. Assess whether its financing, operations, culture and governance match that stage. You will quickly see where performance can be strengthened.
3. **Build your generalist capability.** Each month, choose one area – finance, operations, risk, product, ESG, strategy – and deepen your understanding. The cumulative effect over a year is enormous.
4. **Share the model.** Use it with your team, in interviews, in planning sessions. Use it to challenge old thinking and pass it on. I want

The Standard Model for Business to help as many people as possible. That is why free resources can be accessed at Standardmodelforbusiness.com. Tell your friends and colleagues. The more you and others use the model, the more valuable it becomes.

5. **Take the next step in your development.** Visit Standardmodelforbusiness.com. Join the community. Explore the training courses. Download the resources. This is your journey; equip yourself properly for it.

Contact details

I always enjoy hearing from readers, leaders, professionals and entrepreneurs using The Standard Model for Business in their teams and careers. You can reach me at:

🌐 Standardmodelforbusiness.com

in www.linkedin.com/in/edward-rowe-1271001b6

I welcome your feedback, questions, stories and reflections. Your experience will help shape future editions, new tools and future books as I build the wider Standard Model Universe.

Final note

If you have reached this point, thank you. Writing this book has been one of the most challenging and rewarding experiences of my career. I hope it has given you clarity, confidence and a model you can use for the rest of your professional life.

The future belongs to those who understand how business really works. Now you do. Know business better, do better business.

Go and do something remarkable.

Ed.

Notes

1 J Immelt (attributed), exact source not located. Widely attributed in leadership discussions
2 L Gerstner (attributed), exact source not located. Frequently cited in leadership commentary
3 PF Drucker (attributed), exact source not located. Commonly cited in leadership discussions
4 D Epstein, *Range: How generalists triumph in a specialized world* (Riverhead Books, 2019)
5 Development Dimensions International (DDI), 'Global Leadership Forecast 2018: 25 research findings about the state, context, and future of leadership' (2018), www.ddi.com/research/global-leadership-forecast-2018, accessed 7 January 2026

6 EL Botelho, KR Powell and N Wong, 'The Fastest Path to the CEO Job, According to a 10-Year Study', *Harvard Business Review* (31 January 2018), https://hbr.org/2018/01/the-fastest-path-to-the-ceo-job-according-to-a-10-year-study, accessed 27 January 2026

7 EP Lazear, 'Entrepreneurship', National Bureau of Economic Research, Working Paper No. w9109 (2002), https://ssrn.com/abstract=324051, accessed 28 January 2026

8 M Stuetzer, M Obschonka and E Schmitt-Rodermund, 'Balanced skills among nascent entrepreneurs', MPRA Paper No. 37549 (22 March 2012), https://mpra.ub.uni-muenchen.de/37549, accessed 27 January 2026

9 E Melero and N Palomeras, 'The Renaissance of the *Renaissance Man*?: Specialists vs. Generalists in Teams of Inventors', Universidad Carlos III de Madrid (2012), https://e-archivo.uc3m.es/bitstreams/bfafd1a9-1384-42e2-8286-e6964cb3b7b0/download, accessed 27 January 2026

10 OC Tanner Institute, '2023 Global Culture Report' (2023), www.octanner.com/en-gb/global-culture-report-executive-summary/2023, accessed 7 January 2026

11 E Ries, *The Lean Startup: How today's entrepreneurs use continuous innovation to create radically successful businesses* (Crown Business, 2011)

12 SpaceX, www.spacex.com, accessed 8 December 2025

13 D Simester, 'Why Great New Products Fail', *MIT Sloan Management Review* (15 March 2016), https://sloanreview.mit.edu/article/why-great-new-products-fail, accessed 7 January 2026

14 N Siggelkow and C Terwiesch, 'The Age of Continuous Connection', *Harvard Business Review* (May–June 2019), https://hbr.org/2019/05/the-age-of-continuous-connection, accessed 7 January 2026

15 S Sinek, *Start With Why: How great leaders inspire everyone to take action* (Penguin, 2009)

16 S Michel, DE Bowen and R Johnston, 'Why service recovery fails: Tensions among customer, employee, and process perspectives', *Journal of Service Management*, 20/3 (2009), 253–273, http://dx.doi.org/10.1108/09564230910964381

17 PD Kimmel, JJ Weygandt and DE Kieso, *Financial Accounting: Tools for business decision making*, 9th edn (Wiley, 2018)

18 P Atrill and E McLaney, *Accounting and Finance for Non-Specialists*, 11th edn (Pearson, 2019)

19 Shumpeter, 'Will the mega-merger wave destroy value for shareholders?', *The Economist* (4 December 2025), www.economist.com/business/2025/12/04/will-the-mega-merger-wave-destroy-value-for-shareholders, accessed 12 January 2026

20 ME Porter, *Competitive Advantage: Creating and sustaining superior performance* (Free Press, 1985)
21 ME Porter and C van der Linde, 'Toward a new conception of the environment–competitiveness relationship', *Journal of Economic Perspectives*, 9/4 (1995), 97–118, www.aeaweb.org/articles?id=10.1257/jep.9.4.97, accessed 27 January 2026
22 International Organization for Standardization (ISO), 'About ISO' (n.d.), www.iso.org/about-us.html, accessed 9 December 2025
23 International Organization for Standardization (ISO), 'ISO 9001:2015 Quality management systems — Requirements' (2015), www.iso.org/standard/62085.html, accessed 9 December 2025
24 International Organization for Standardization (ISO), 'ISO 45001:2018 Occupational health and safety management systems — Requirements with guidance for use' (2018), www.iso.org/standard/63787.html, accessed 9 December 2025
25 International Organization for Standardization (ISO), 'ISO 14001:2015 Environmental management systems — Requirements with guidance for use' (2015), www.iso.org/standard/60857.html, accessed 9 December 2025
26 International Organization for Standardization (ISO), 'ISO 50001:2018 Energy management systems — Requirements with guidance for use' (2018), www.iso.org/standard/69426.html, accessed 9 December 2025

27 WE Deming, *Out of the Crisis* (MIT Press, 1986)
28 International Organization for Standardization (ISO), 'ISO 31000:2018 Risk management — Guidelines' (2018), www.iso.org/iso-31000-risk-management.html, accessed 27 January 2026
29 DW Hubbard, *The Failure of Risk Management: Why it's broken and how to fix it*, 2nd edn (Wiley, 2020)
30 Global Reporting Initiative (GRI), 'Getting started' (2021), www.globalreporting.org/how-to-use-the-gri-standards, accessed 9 December 2025
31 Sustainability Accounting Standards Board, 'SASB Standards overview' (2018), www.sasb.org/standards, accessed 9 December 2025
32 Task Force on Climate-related Financial Disclosures, 'Final Report: Recommendations of the Task Force on Climate-related Financial Disclosures' (June 2017), www.fsb.org/uploads/P290617-5.pdf, accessed 12 January 2026
33 European Commission, 'Corporate sustainability reporting' (9 December 2025), https://finance.ec.europa.eu/capital-markets-union-and-financial-markets/company-reporting-and-auditing/company-reporting/corporate-sustainability-reporting_en, accessed 9 December 2025
34 EFRAG, 'Sustainability reporting' (2023), www.efrag.org/en/sustainability-reporting, accessed 12 January 2026

35 The Institute of Internal Auditors (IIA) (2017), 'International Professional Practices Framework (IPPF) for internal auditing' (n.d.), www.theiia.org/en/standards, accessed 9 December 2025

36 Institute of Internal Auditors (IIA), 'The IIA's Three Lines Model: An update of the Three Lines of Defense' (8 September 2020), www.theiia.org/en/content/position-papers/2020/the-iias-three-lines-model-an-update-of-the-three-lines-of-defense, accessed 13 January 2026

37 S Blank and B Dorf, *The Startup Owner's Manual: The step-by-step guide for building a great company* (K&S Ranch, 2012)

38 B Feld and J Mendelson, *Venture Deals: Be smarter than your lawyer and venture capitalist*, 4th edn (Wiley, 2016)

39 R Hoffman and C Yeh, *Blitzscaling: The lightning-fast path to building massively valuable companies* (Crown Currency, 2018)

40 RA Brealey, SC Myers and F Allen, *Principles of Corporate Finance*, 13th edn (McGraw-Hill Education, 2020)

41 JR Ritter and I Welch, 'A review of IPO activity, pricing, and allocations', *The Journal of Finance*, 57/4 (2002), 1795–1828, https://doi.org/10.1111/1540-6261.00478

42 CB Insights, 'The Top 12 Reasons Startups Fail' (3 August 2021), www.cbinsights.com/research/startup-failure-reasons-top, accessed 27 January 2026

Acknowledgements

Writing *The Standard Model for Business* has been both a challenge and a privilege. This book could not have been completed without the encouragement, guidance and inspiration of many people along the way.

I am deeply grateful to my family. To Kristina, my wife, for her patience and unwavering belief in me throughout the long hours of writing. To my children – William, Maria and Olivia – who remind me daily of why curiosity, learning and perseverance matter. Their love and support have been my greatest source of energy.

I owe special thanks to the many colleagues, mentors and peers across the companies and industries I have worked in. Their insights, challenges and shared experiences helped shape the practical framework you see in this book. I am grateful to those who have trusted me with leadership opportunities, encouraged my ideas and pushed me to think critically about how businesses operate, grow, stabilise and ultimately thrive.

I would also like to thank my publisher, Rethink Press, for believing in this project and for guiding me through the process of turning a framework into a book that can serve readers at every stage of their business journey.

Finally, I want to acknowledge the countless professionals and entrepreneurs who inspired me throughout my career with their questions and struggles. This book is, in many ways, written for you; to provide a model that makes sense of the challenges of understanding business and to serve as a compass when the path forward is unclear.

The Author

Edward Rowe is a governance, assurance and risk executive with more than twenty-one years of experience advising boards, investment leaders and executive teams across Europe, the Middle East, Southeast Asia and the United States. A Fellow Chartered Accountant (ICAEW), his career spans financial services, global manufacturing, sovereign wealth and private equity, giving him a uniquely broad lens on how organisations grow, adapt and succeed.

Ed began his career at Grant Thornton, where he built his foundations in assurance, risk and internal control. He later joined KPMG's Audit Committee

Institute, advising non-executive directors on governance responsibilities, risk oversight and the practical realities of corporate accountability. These early roles shaped his belief that good governance is not a technical exercise but a leadership discipline that underpins long-term performance.

His career accelerated when he moved into industry as Group Assurance Manager for a multinational distribution group operating across Western Europe, where he built and led the internal audit function. In 2010, Ed relocated to Abu Dhabi, joining one of the world's most sophisticated sovereign wealth platforms. Over the next fifteen years, he delivered assurance and risk oversight across portfolios that included aerospace, advanced manufacturing, renewables, technology, mining, financial services, healthcare and global investment vehicles.

Ed has led and managed complex audit programmes, overseen assurance activities across multi-billion-dollar investment portfolios and worked closely with audit, risk and compliance committees to strengthen governance across diverse organisations. His work has taken him inside semiconductor fabrication plants, renewable energy projects, high-growth technology companies and international investment platforms, giving him a rare, behind-the-scenes view of how strategy, risk, culture and execution work in the real world.

Today, Ed is responsible for building the internal audit and risk management functions for a sovereign private equity firm with over $400 billion in assets under management. He continues to advise senior leaders on governance, risk, culture and organisational maturity, the pillars that inspired The Standard Model for Business.

Across two decades and multiple industries, Ed observed a recurring challenge: talented professionals often lack a simple, universal way to understand how businesses actually work. The Standard Model for Business was born from his desire to solve that problem, not through theory but through the practical clarity gained from years inside boardrooms, investment reviews and complex organisational environments.

Ed lives in Abu Dhabi with his wife, Kristina, and their three children. When he isn't writing or advising leaders, he enjoys spending time with his family, reading, architecture, high-fidelity audio, exploring new ideas and building the growing ecosystem around The Standard Model for Business.

Standardmodelforbusiness.com

www.ingramcontent.com/pod-product-compliance
Lightning Source LLC
LaVergne TN
LVHW052303100826
845147LV00006B/665

* 9 7 8 1 7 8 1 3 3 9 7 8 7 *